Republic of Korea

The Asia and the Pacific Intra-regional Outbound Series

Republic of Korea – The Asia and the Pacific Intra-reginal Outbound Series
ISBN-13: 978-92-844-1126-9

Published and printed by the World Tourism Organization, Madrid, Spain
First printing 2007

The designations employed and the presentation of material in this publication do not imply the expression of any opinions whatsoever on the part of the Secretariat of the World Tourism Organization concerning the legal status of any country, territory, city or area, or of its authorities or concerning the delimitation of its frontiers or boundaries.

World Tourism Organization
Calle Capitán Haya, 42
28020 Madrid, Spain
Tel.: (+34) 915 678 100
Fax: (+34) 915 713 733
Website: www.unwto.org
Email: omt@unwto.org

Table of Contents

Foreword

The Asia-Pacific region by the very nature of its surface area, population, cultural diversity, and economic activity is a vast store house of tourism. For too long the region has been associated with inbound tourism but a closer analysis shows that the outbound potential and growth rates are far superior to that of the other economic blocs of the world whether it be Europe or the Americas.

The UNWTO 2020 market survey predicts that China will be the leading inbound and the fourth largest outbound destination with 100 million tourists. Recent trends in the outbound figures of China indicate that this figure will be surpassed earlier than estimated. Another UNWTO survey has placed China and India amongst the fastest growing outbound destinations with growth around 10% per year.

A very interesting feature of the Asia-Pacific outbound statistics reveals that 78% of outbound Asian traffic is to the region itself. Intra-regional traffic therefore plays a very important role in the economic and tourist landscape which is gradually but firmly changing the world tourism scenario.

UNWTO has, therefore, commissioned the present series on "Asia and the Pacific – intra regional outbound" market studies through leading academics of Asia and the Pacific, working on their own or through reputed tourism institutes, to analyse the potential and future trends of seven leading markets viz: Australia, China, Hong Kong, India, Japan, Republic of Korea and Thailand.

It is the beginning of an initiative that hopefully will be continued in the future as more information, data, and research emerge of these outbound markets on the one hand and the efforts made by the inbound destinations to improve their infrastructure and products to receive their "neighbours" on the other.

I congratulate the Regional Representation for Asia and the Pacific of UNWTO for producing these studies.

Francesco Frangialli

Secretary-General
World Tourism Organization

Acknowledgements

This study is a part of the Asia and Pacific intra-regional outbound tourism series, being conducted by the World Tourism Organization. As intra-regional tourism within the Asia-Pacific region is on the rise, and constitutes a good portion of the total tourists to the region, these studies focus on the potential of the Asia-Pacific generating markets, as a source market for the countries concerned.

The World Tourism Organization (UNWTO) hopes that this marketing study will be of benefit to the concerned NTAs, NTOs and other stakeholders in the tourism industry in their endeavour to understand the source market.

We wish to thank Dr. Chulwon Kim from Kyunghee University for undertaking the study.

Mr. Omar Nawaz and Ms. Lorna Hartantyo, under the supervision of Mr. Xu Jing of UNWTO, are responsible for coordinating and editing the study.

This study is produced by the Regional Representation for Asia and the Pacific of UNWTO, in collaboration with the Market Intelligence and Promotion Department of UNWTO.

Executive Summary

The population of the Republic of Korea was estimated at around 48.8 million. The Republic of Korea is a highly urbanized country with 87% of its population living in urban areas. The Metropolitan area encompasses the capital city, Seoul, Incheon Metropolitan City and Kyonggi Province, and its population is estimated at around 22.6 million, or 48% of the total population of the country. The Republic of Korea is the 10th biggest economy in the world, with a GDP of US$ 787.5 billion.

Along with the liberalization and internationalization that has led to an increase in income levels and wealth of the Korean people, more and more Koreans travel abroad for sightseeing or for business purposes. The close proximity of the Asian-Pacific countries to the Republic of Korea is a leading factor in the increase of outbound traffic from the Republic of Korea.

Korean overseas departures in 2005 reached a record high of 10 million, an increase of 14.2% over the previous year.

Factors affecting the growth in outbound tourism included a strong Korean Won and an increase in leisure time due to the official implementation of a national five-day workweek. The favorite travel destinations of Koreans in Asia are: China (2,960,642), Japan (1,739,424), Thailand (661,779), Philippines (481,397) and Hong Kong (344,393). Visits grew 31.9% for Thailand and 27.6% for Philippines.

Information sources affecting outbound travel decisions of the Koreans include travel agencies, internet searches, and recommendations by friends. When thinking about traveling abroad, rather than focusing purely on the cost issue Koreans now appear to be more concerned whether the trip is worth the price. Before choosing a destination, Koreans learn about the details of the trip, through various channels such as internet, points of views of friends, travel agencies. These sources of information help them make their decisions on whether the destination offers the best value for money.

Natural sceneries and local cultures are what attract the Korean travellers. In the meantime, relaxation and shopping are gradually becoming two other important decision factors for the travellers, as more and more Koreans need an escape from the hectic city life. Therefore, when preparing a trip, they would mostly ask questions about the availability of sightseeing, shopping, entertainment, and variety of restaurants at the destinations. Korean outbound travellers are generally satisfied with the available tour guides and services they have experienced while traveling abroad. Satisfaction has remained relatively stable since 2001. However, the degree of satisfaction reported is lower than that for accommodations, food and dining, and shopping goods.

Korean outbound travellers have also reported language as the major inconvenience in overseas travel. Food was also an important factor. But these numbers have decreased substantially since 1997. In 2005 all types of travel inconveniences are reported at a lower frequency.

There are no distinct seasonal variations in the Republic of Korea's outbound travel market. However, the months of July and August, which coincides with the period of the summer vacation, has the most number of overseas travels every year.

Korean outbound travellers increasingly prefer package tours. Currently, over 60% of outbound travellers purchase packaged tours. Koreans generally spend money on shopping while they are abroad. The majority choose to shop in duty-free shops. In 2005, almost 82% of the travellers have reported shopping at duty free shops.

Finally, cooperation of the NTO with travel companies and airlines is necessary for successfully marketing a destination.

Chapter 1

Overview of the Republic of Korea

1.1 Demography and Geography

The population of the Republic of Korea as of 2004 was 48,199,227. The population density of the country is 490 persons per km². The rapid growth of the population was once a serious social problem in the Republic of Korea, as in most other developing nations. Due to successful family planning campaigns and changing attitudes, population growth has curbed remarkably in recent years. A notable trend in the population structure is that it is getting increasingly older. The 2003 population estimation revealed that 8.3% of the total population was 65 years old or over. The number of people in the age group of 15 to 64 years accounted for 71.44%.

At the administrative level, the country consists of nine provinces; the capital city of Seoul; and six metropolitan cities: Busan, Daegu, Incheon, Gwangju, Daejeon and Ulsan. In total, there are 77 cities and 88 counties. The Republic of Korea is a highly urbanized country with 87% of its population living in urban areas. The Metropolitan area (known as 'Sudokwon' in Korean) encompasses the capital city, Seoul, Incheon Metropolitan City and Gyonggi Province. This region includes 48%, or 22.6 million, of the population. The following map depicts the Republic of Korea in terms of administrative areas and the nation's location from a regional perspective. Seoul, the capital of the Republic of Korea, in which more than 10 million of the country's 48 million population call home, has grown into a global metropolis housing a bigger portion of its country's population than that of New York, London or Tokyo. This represents a higher population density than metropolitan areas of other countries. People living in the metropolitan area in and around London or Paris comprise less than 20% of the total population. People living in Tokyo and its surrounding areas, account for about 32% of Japan's total population.

In addition, the metropolitan area around Seoul currently houses about 84% of government bodies and institutions, 88% of the Republic of Korea's 30 largest companies, and 65% of the 20 most popular universities in the nation. More than 65% of all bank transactions, both savings and lending, take place in Seoul.

Koreans are one ethnic family and speak one language. Sharing distinct physical characteristics, they are believed to be descendants of several Mongol tribes that migrated onto the Korean Peninsula from Central Asia.

The Republic of Korea is situated on the Korean Peninsula, which spans 1,100 km north to south. The Korean Peninsula lies on the northeastern section of the Asian continent. The peninsula shares its northern border with China and Russia. To its east is the East Sea, beyond which neighboring Japan lies. In addition to the mainland peninsula, the Republic of Korea includes some 3,000 islands. The Republic of Korea encompasses a total of 222,154 km², almost the same size as Britain or Romania.

1.2 Economy

The Republic of Korea is the 10th biggest economy in the world with a gross domestic product (GDP) of US$ 787.5 billion (2005 preliminary findings). The National Accounts in the year 2005 (preliminary) reported the Republic of Korea's real gross domestic product (GDP) up 4% in 2005 (Bank of Korea, 2006). The slightly higher than expected GDP growth was driven by robust exports, a pick-up in private consumption and accelerating corporate investments. The nation's GDP growth is expected to achieve the 5% level in 2006, close to its growth potential. The Gross National Income (GDI) per capita, which can serve as a rough indicator of purchasing power, in 2005 was 7,875 million Won. In 2000, it was 6,842 million Won or US$ 4,820 (Bank of Korea). GDP growth in (%) from 2000 to 2005 is illustrated in the following figure:

GDP Growth, 2000-2005 (%)

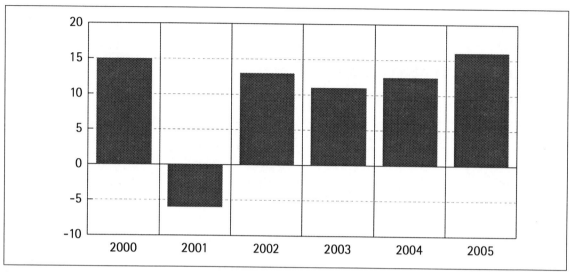

Source: Bank of Korea (2006)

The sharp appreciation of the Korean Won is the main factor for the growth of the Republic of Korea's GDP. Since 2003, the Korean currency has been sharply appreciated. This will be a key factor affecting a growing number of Koreans traveling overseas.

1.3 Holidays

July 1, 2005 marked the inauguration of the Republic of Korea's five-day workweek. This policy goes into effect for employees in public service, finance organizations, and large enterprises. National tourism and leisure patterns are expected to change considerably as family travel during the longer weekend increases. Major changes in the Republic of Korea's tourism industry are predicted as the five-day workweek takes hold nationwide.

Early on, the Republic of Korea used a lunar calendar, as did most agrarian societies. As the rest of the world encroached on the Republic of Korea, it eventually went to the solar calendar. Yet the majority of the country still uses the lunar calendar to keep track of births and deaths and some traditional holidays. Many people celebrate their birthdays according to both calendars, and the first day of each calendar is a national holiday.

There are 11 holidays every year as follows: New Year's Day, Lunar New Year (*Seol-nal*), Independence Movement Day, Arbor Day, Buddha's Birthday, Children's Day, Memorial Day, Liberation Day, Thanksgiving Day *(Chuseok)*, National Foundation Day, Christmas. In particular, holidays by the lunar calendar are New Year's (*Seol-nal*): 1st day of 1st month, plus the day before and after; Buddha's Birthday *(Seokka Tanshin-il):* 8th day of 4th month; and Harvest Moon Festival *(Chuesok):* 14th to 16th day of 8th month.

Holidays	Date
New Year's Day	1 January
Lunar New Year (Seol-nal)*	Lunar 1 January
Independence Movement Day (Samiljeol)	1 March
Arbor Day	5 April
Buddha's Birthday	Lunar 8 April
Children's Day	5 May
Memorial Day	6 June
Liberation Day	15 August
Thanksgiving Day (Chuseok)*	15 Lunar August
National Foundation Day	3 October
Christmas	25 December

* Three-day holiday.
Source: http://www.korea.net

Chapter 2

The Republic of Korea as
an Outbound Tourism Market

2.1 Development of the Outbound Korean Traveller

The number of Koreans traveling overseas has seen a rapid growth after the liberalization of overseas travel, which was introduced in 1986 when Korean overseas tourists totaled 450,000. However, due to the influence of the International Monetary Fund (IMF) crisis in 1998, overseas travel was diminished and hence outbound traffic in 1998 plummeted by some 32.5% to 3.07 million. Thanks to the gradual recovery of the Korean economy in 1999, the number of outbound travellers rapidly rose by 41.6% to 4.34 million.

Tourism is an important industry for the Republic of Korea. In the past few years tourism has grown despite a series of unprecedented global disasters, and international tourist arrivals exceeded 600 million in spite of natural disasters and rising fuel costs. The number of incoming tourists to the Republic of Korea grew by 3.5% and most tourists were from other Asian countries. Koreans traveling abroad reached 10,077,619, a record high thanks to a strong currency exchange rate favoring the Korean Won against the US dollar. Most Koreans visited Asian destinations. Total tourism revenues in 2005 reached US$ 5.6 billion (preliminary finding), a decrease of 6.7% over the previous year but expenditures still continued to rise, outrunning revenue, finishing the year at a 65% deficit. Outbound tourists outnumbered inbound by one and a half time, and Koreans spent more overseas than tourists spent in their visits to the Republic of Korea. This is probably due to the growing exchange value of the Korean won.

Internal tourism grew strongly due to developing infrastructure and services such as the KTX fast train, and the emergence and growth of various special interest tourism products. These tourism products were successful because of certain strong promotional strategies and the implementation of a national five-day workweek.

In summary, the tourism industry is very important to the Republic of Korea's economy and is continuing to grow. Various economic and social effects will become more visible as this trend continues.

Growth of Korean Outbound Tourism, 1986-2005

Year	Outbound Tourists	Growth Rate (%)	Permitted Age to Travel Abroad
1986	454,974	-0.6	> 50
1987	510,538	12.2	> 45
1988	725,176	42.0	> 40 > 30
1989	1,213,112	67.3	Abolished age limit
1990	1,560,923	28.7	–
1991	1,856,923	19.0	–
1992	2,043,299	10.0	–
1993	2,419,930	18.4	–
1994	3,154,326	30.3	–
1995	3,818,740	21.1	–

© 2007 World Tourism Organization – ISBN 978-92-844-1126-9

Year	Outbound Tourists	Growth Rate (%)	Permitted Age to Travel Abroad
1996	4,649,251	21.7	–
1997	4,542,159	-2.3	–
1998	3,066,926	-32.5	–
1999	4,341,546	41.6	–
2000	5,508,242	26.9	–
2001	6,084,476	10.5	–
2002	7,123,407	17.1	–
2003	7,086,133	-0.5	–
2004	8,825,585	24.5	–
2005	10,077,619	14.2	–

Source: Ministry of Culture and Tourism

2.2 Volume of Outbound Korean Traveller

Korean overseas departures in 2005 reached a record high of 10,077,619, an increase of 14.2% over the previous year. Factors affecting this growth included a strong Korean Won and an increase in leisure time due to the official implementation of a national five-day workweek in 2005. The favorite travel destinations of Koreans in Asia are: China (2,960,642), Japan (1,739,424), Thailand (661,779), Philippines (481,397) and Hong Kong (344,393). Visitation grew 31.9% for Thailand and 27.6% for the Philippines. In the Americas, Korean tourists visited the USA (665,181), Canada (134,975), and Brazil (4,321). Visitation grew 14.8% for Brazil from 3,763 to 4.321. In Europe, Korean tourists visited England (116,224), Germany (141,606), and the Netherlands (39,542). The Netherlands recorded the highest growth in visitation, 51.2%. The Republic of Korea's outbound market is listed in the table below for the years 1997 to 2005.

Destination for Korean Overseas Departures, 1997-2005 (%)

Ranking	Country	1997	1999	2001	2003	2005
1	China	20.3	27.7	32.5	25.2	34.7
2	Japan	32.1	30.5	26.0	24.2	19.1
3	USA	10.3	8.0	11.6	12.0	7.6
4	Thailand	8.8	11.1	3.5	9.2	7.0
5	Philippines	4.3	0.8	3.2	4.5	4.9

Source: Analysis from Korea Tourism Organization's (KTO) raw data (2006)

Countries in Asia Visited by Koreans, 2005 (%)

China	34.7
Japan	19.1
USA	7.6
Thailand	7.0
Philippines	4.9

Source: Analysis from KTO's raw data (2006)

2.3 Revenues and Expenditures in Tourism

In the Republic of Korea, tourism revenue for 2004 was US$ 5.7 billion, a 6.6% growth from 2003, while expenditure was US$ 9.5 billion, a 15.2% increase from 2003. The balance was minus US$ 3.8 billion, a 30.9% deficit in comparison with the previous year.

The number of outbound Korean travellers in 2004 was about 8,830,000 whereas 5,820,000 foreigners visit the Republic of Korea. Tourism expenditure increased, as the amount spent by each Korean traveling overseas averaged US$ 1,169 compared to US$ 1,045 spent by each foreign visitor to the Republic of Korea, a difference of US$ 124.

It is known that the stronger Korean Won reduced the purchasing power of foreigners visiting the Republic of Korea, directly affecting how much they spent on shopping, meanwhile increasing the purchasing power of the Koreans traveling overseas (Ministry of Culture and Tourism, 2005). It is estimated that tourism revenue in the Republic of Korea for 2005 decreased by 6.7% from the previous year to US$ 5.6 billion and tourism expenditures increased by 21.2% to US$ 11.9 billion, yielding an annual deficit of US$ 6.2 billion, an increase of 65.5% in comparison with the previous year. The per capita amount spent by outbound Korean tourists averaged US$ 1,239 (US$ 1,169 in 2004) compared with the average US$ 944 (US$ 1,045 in 2004) spent by inbound tourists visiting the Republic of Korea, a difference of US$ 295 (US$ 124 in 2004). It is assumed that the stronger Korean Won reduced purchasing power of the foreigners visiting the Republic of Korea but increased the purchasing power of Koreans traveling overseas. Details of the Korean tourism revenue and expenditure for 2004 and 2005 are summarized in the table and figure below:

Tourism Revenue and Expenditure, 2004 and 2005

Year	Revenue		Expenditure		Balance		Revenue		Expenditure	
	US$ million	+/- (%)	US$ million	+/- (%)	US$ million	+/- (%)	Per capita (US$)	+/- (%)	Per capita (US$)	+/- (%)
2004	6,053.1	13.3	9,856.4	19.5	-3,803.3	30.9	1,045	-7.4	1,169	-4.5
2005	5,649.8	-6.7	11,942.7	21.2	-6.292.9	65.5	944	-9.7	1,239	6.0

Note: % means variation from previous year
Source: KTO (2006) Statistical data. 2004 data is confirmed, but 2005 data is estimated.

2.4 Propensity to Travel

Koreans' desire to visit a foreign country is illustrated in the table and figure below. The most desirable country to visit is Japan, followed closely by the United States of America. These two leading destinations switched first and second places in 2005. The 19 most desired destinations are found in the subsequent table, as well as 9 of the most desired destinations for the years 1997 to 2005.

List of Most Desirable Destination to Visit, 1997-2005 (%)

Desire to Visit	2005	2003	2001	1999	1997
Japan	28.3	27.3	25.9	31.4	27.6
USA	24.8	28.0	32.5	43.5	42.7
Australia	21.1	22.2	24.6	39.4	43.8
France	19.1	19.4	17.8	27.4	26.2
England	16.6	13.6	11.7	17.8	18.6
China	16.4	22.6	19.3	22.8	20.1

Desire to Visit	2005	2003	2001	1999	1997
Canada	13.2	17.4	19.0	28.1	26.0
Switzerland	13.1	11.9	15.5	–	–
Italy	10.8	10.6	11.4	26.9	23.7
Thailand	9.5	7.1	6.2	5.8	5.6
Germany	9.5	6.5	6.3	12.5	14.3
Hawaii	8.5	9.3	–	–	–
New Zealand	8.2	8.5	9.9	21.8	20.1
Guam/Saipan	7.8	6.0	9.0	9.1	10.5
Hong Kong	6.1	8.7	9.2	11.0	9.8
Singapore	5.9	5.1	6.1	12.3	14.2
Netherlands	5.8	5.1	6.3	11.5	11.0
Greece	5.8	3.8	3.6	–	–
Vietnam	5.7	1.9	3.5	–	–

Source: KTO (2005)

2.5 Profile of Outbound Travellers from the Republic of Korea

Market segmentation for Korean outbound travellers reveals a number of interesting characteristics of the Korean outbound market. Namely, a larger number of female Koreans are traveling, so as the elderly.

2.5.1 Gender

The following table summarizes Korean departures by gender from 2000 to 2004. This table indicates that the number in 2004 of male tourists has risen by 24.5% and the number of female tourists has risen by 28.9%. More female Koreans are traveling. The figure below illustrates the total departures of males and females. This trend can be explained as housewives (they may be classified as unemployed people) tend to travel more, with their social groups as they have more spare time than men. This market consists of housewives who are financially stable.

Korean Departures by Gender, 2000-2004

Year	Total	Male	Female
2000	5,508,242	2,874,990	2,633,252
2001	6,084,476	3,186,211	2,215,323
2002	7,123,407	3,725,611	2,649,766
2003	7,086,133	3,761,865	2,581,517
2004	8,825,585	4,682,344	3,326,559

Source: KTO (2005)

2.5.2 Occupation

The following table shows Korean departures by occupation since 2002 and reveals that the fastest growth by market segment are people with "no employment" – which in 2004 are basically housewives (34.1%), followed by those employed in the public service sector (27.2%). The figure thereafter indicates the departures graphically from 1985 to 2004.

Korean Departures by Occupation, 2002-2005

Category	2002 Number	2002 +/- (%)	2003 Number	2003 +/- (%)	2004 Number	2004 +/- (%)	2005 Number	2005 +/- (%)
Official	85,053	28.5	93,753	10.2	119,286	27.2	131,186	10.0
White Collar	2,447,761	18.2	2,495,646	2.0	3,037,773	21.7	3,351,484	10.3
Businessmen	488,352	11.1	479,834	-1.7	604,647	26.0	687,867	13.8
Professor	175,061	17.6	186,821	6.7	233,151	24.8	261,579	12.2
Student	792,354	21.1	842,765	6.4	1,037,136	23.1	1,203,829	16.1
Others	626,825	54.7	565,334	-9.8	636,636	12.6	636,668	0.01
Unemployed	2,077,641	19.8	1,979,184	-4.7	2,654,005	34.1	3,225,836	21.5

Note: % means variation from previous year
Source: KTO (2005)

2.5.3 Age

The following table indicates that those in the elderly and aging strata (those in their 50s and 60s) enjoy a relatively greater growth of 33.9% and 31.6% in 2004 correspondingly. They have more free time and affluent financial resources, compared to other age groups. Interestingly, Korean traditional filial duty derived from Confucianism and tends to affect the increasing number of over 60s aging strata in overseas travel, although this aging strata, partly, has more free time and money after their retirement. The figure below illustrates the growth of tourist departures by age group.

Korean Departures by Age Group, 2001-2005

Category	2001 Number	2002 Number	2002 +/- (%)	2003 Number	2003 +/- (%)	2004 Number	2004 +/- (%)	2005 Number	2005 +/- (%)
0 – 20	569,750	691,961	21.4	729,694	5.5	906,752	24.3	1,092,317	20.5
21 – 30	1,133,723	1,261,619	11.3	1,213,199	-3.8	1,490,654	22.9	1,698,122	13.9
31 – 40	1,444,958	1,665,648	15.3	1,640,473	-1.5	1,987,184	21.1	2,217,221	11.6
41 – 50	1,268,030	1,550,554	22.3	1,592,735	+2.7	1,986,780	24.7	2,251,420	13.3
51 – 60	766,182	897,515	17.1	881,823	-1.7	1,180,754	33.9	1,386,000	17.4
>61	513,670	625,732	21.8	585,413	-6.4	770,510	31.6	880,961	14.3

Note: % means variation from previous year
Source: KTO (2005)

2.6 Consumer Behavior Pattern on Outbound Tourism

Outbound travel reached a record high for multiple trips in 1999 followed by a slump in 2001, and has slowly increased since then. However, single trips have followed a different trend, slowly decreasing since recovering from a slump in 1999. Generally, close to half the outbound traffic from the Republic of Korea is in terms of four or more trips per year. It could be assumed that the majority of the Korean outbound market consists of travellers for pleasure.

The major information sources affecting the outbound travel decision are traditionally the recommendations of others, but the internet has increased dramatically in recent years as a major factor. Travel agencies have enjoyed a moderately increasing effect on the travel decision. This may be related to the current role of the internet, as more and more travel agencies in the Republic of Korea are moving to an e-business model.

Decision factors concerning outbound travel are largely affected by travel agency advertising, possibly due to the increased presence of special package deals or discounts. Recommendations and business factors have decreased in the past two years.

The experiences of Korean tourists in foreign countries have been ranging from business related activities such as industry inspection (down from 1997) to leisure pursuits such as sightseeing and amusement. Shopping has been a relatively stable activity over time. Outbound travellers increasingly prefer packaged tours. In 1997 Koreans equally preferred FIT and package tours but by 2005 this has changed to about 60% preferring packaged tours.

Demographic changes in the outbound travel market influence the ways and reasons of Korean travel. Accordingly, spending by group travellers has risen over the past eight years as well as spending for sports and leisure activities. A general decrease in the total cost of package travel has occurred, probably due to the increase in sales volume. Koreans traveling abroad generally spend money on shopping. Shopping occurs most commonly in duty free shops, followed by shops and stores in general or souvenir shops.

The increase of travellers shopping at souvenir shops could be attributed to the increase in package tours, which usually would include a routine stop at such venues. Souvenirs, cosmetics, foods and alcohol are the four most frequently purchased items. Traditionally, only cosmetics and alcohol were purchased, but as these items become more available domestically, travellers turn their spending power to local products and foods.

2.6.1 Purpose of Visit

Outbound tourists reported their reasons for traveling as: "pleasure-purpose" (54.8% or 5,521,044 people), "business-purpose" (7.6% or 2,074,964), or "visit relatives and friends (VFR)-purpose" (865,828). Compared to 2004, "pleasure-purpose", "business-purpose", and "visit relatives and friends" tourists increased by 18.0%, 7.6%, and 22.8% respectively. Reasons for traveling are listed below for the years 1997 to 2005.

Purpose of Outbound Travel, 1997-2005 (%)

Travel Purpose	1997	1999	2001	2003	2005
Tourism	32.6	24.7	62.0	50.4	61.4
Business	28.6	36.2	16.3	23.6	21.6
Visitation	12.0	12.4	10.5	9.7	7.7
Training	11.8	5.2	5.8	5.7	4.7
Honeymoon	3.5	5.9	1.8	4.8	–
Conference/Exhibition	6.8	9.0	1.8	2.9	–

Travel Purpose	1997	1999	2001	2003	2005
Cultural/Sports activity	1.9	0.9	0.8	1.7	–
Religion/Pilgrimage	–	–	–	–	3.6
Other	2.8	5.7	1.0	1.2	1.0
Total	100.0	100.0	100.0	100.0	100.0

Source : Analysis from KTO's raw data (2006)

The travel activities of Koreans while abroad include a wide variety of sightseeing, amusement, leisure sports and shopping. But shopping and sightseeing are the most frequently reported activities.

Experiences in Foreign Countries, 1997-2005 (%)

Tourist Experiences	1997	1999	2001	2003	2005
Sightseeing of Natural Scenery and Attractions	70.5	63.7	86.7	85.7	97.6
City Sightseeing	61.9	66.8	90.5	91.6	93.8
Shopping	–	–	93.3	88.5	93.6
Visiting Historic Places	52.9	47.4	59.0	49.0	74.5
Amusement/Entertainment/Self-Actualization	19.6	15.8	27.7	46.7	35.4
Festival/Ethnic Events	19.8	17.8	19.8	22.8	18.1
Swimming/Bathe in the Sea	18.5	19.5	11.6	12.5	17.2
Spa and Recreation	13.0	11.2	14.4	10.2	15.3
Industry inspection	24.2	28.0	8.3	6.3	13.9
Climbing/Camping/Hiking	7.3	6.4	8.6	5.5	6.4
Golfing	3.0	3.1	3.2	2.4	3.9
Casino	4.1	2.8	2.03	3.9	3.0
Skiing	1.1	0.3	0.7	0.4	1.0
Other	–	–	0.5	0.8	0.6

Source: Analysis from KTO's raw data (2006)

2.6.2 Seasonality

The outbound traffic by season shows that August and July, the summer vacation period, is the peak season to travel and that January, the winter vacation period, recorded relatively higher departures, compared to other months. It is recognized that there are no distinct seasonal variations in the Republic of Korea's outbound travel market. In 2003, the months of March, April, and May marked a relatively lower number of Korean outbound travellers compared to other months, but these variations were not repeated in 2004. It would seem that Koreans tend to travel overseas regardless of monthly seasonality except for the month of October, even though the months of July and August (period of summer vacation) have the most number of overseas travels every year. However, Thanksgiving (Chuseok) holiday also affected outbound travel during the month of October.

Summary of Korean Departures by Month, 1997-2005

	1997	1999	2001	2003	2005
Total	**4,542,159**	**4,341,546**	**5,508,242**	**7,086,133**	**10,077,619**
January	474,389	347,406	454,469	742,059	897,406
February	336,171	275,440	397,303	621,358	745,998
March	358,148	314,865	397,950	519,583	707,058
April	356,446	310,966	407,250	339,384	762,096
May	377,652	347,367	457,930	360,295	802,497
June	394,051	349,227	452,987	483,956	864,057
July	499,030	446,014	589,214	729,135	1,020,757
August	495,884	448,383	571,379	793,315	1,069,400
September	330,778	346,069	430,456	591,030	785,549
October	367,945	386,174	446,588	648,385	848,088
November	336,780	382,580	439,805	640,191	784,032
December	214,885	387,055	462,911	617,442	790,681

Source: KTO (2006)

2.6.3 Frequency of Travel

The frequency of outbound Korean travellers varies by year. The following table provides a summary of the frequency of travel to overseas destinations from 1997 to 2005. The additional figure illustrates this frequency for the same period graphically. The result shows that Koreans tend to take more frequent overseas travel each year, compared to previous years. It is evident that the number of experienced travellers has been increasing.

Frequency of Travel to Overseas Destinations, 1997-2005 (%)

Frequency of Travel	1997	1999	2001	2003	2005
Once	25.2	16.9	28.2	25.4	23.5
Two times	15.0	10.9	20.3	16.2	16.0
Three times	9.8	8.9	12.8	11.5	13.2
More than Four times	50.0	63.3	38.7	46.9	47.3
Total	**100.0**	**100.0**	**100.0**	**100.0**	**100.0**

Source: Analysis from KTO's raw data (2006)

2.6.4 Information Source

Major information sources influencing the outbound travel decisions of Koreans include travel agencies, internet searches and recommendations by others. Koreans want to know more about the details of a trip in advance, through various channels including the internet, friends or agencies, to assist them in making decisions on whether the price paid is worth it. All major information sources below are listed for the years 2001, 2003 and 2005.

Major Information Sources Affecting the Outbound Travel Decision, 2001-2005 (%)

Information Sources	2001	2003	2005
Travel Agency	30.0	25.9	39.5
Internet Search	17.0	28.6	30.7
Recommendation	43.5	38.1	27.5
Guidebook/Travel publications	5.8	4.3	1.7
Mass Media	1.4	1.8	0.3
Embassy	0.5	0.2	0.1
Other	1.8	1.1	0.2
Total	**100.0**	**100.0**	**100.0**

Source: Analysis from KTO's raw data (2006)

2.6.5 Decision Factors

Decision factors for outbound travel closely correspond to available information sources described above. A major difference would be business and curiosity, two factors that surpass internet search as a decision factor. This would indicate that information sources do not solely determine the decision to travel internationally. A detailed list of major decision factors for Korean outbound travellers is provided below for 2003 and 2005.

Decision Factors for Outbound Travel, 2003 and 2005 (%)

Decision Factor	2003	2005
Travel Agency Advertisement	17.2	34.7
Recommendation	33.9	25.2
Business	23.3	13.4
Curiosity to Visit a Foreign Country	11.8	10.9
Internet Search	8.2	7.1
Low Price	2.9	3.0
Training	–	1.9
School Excursion	–	1.7
Destination's PR	2.0	1.5
Mass Media	0.7	0.6
Total	**100.0**	**100.0**

Source: Analysis from KTO's raw data (2006)

2.6.6 Package vs. FIT

Korean outbound travellers increasingly prefer package tours. This development of changing preferences is illustrated below. Currently, over 60% of outbound travellers purchase package tours.

Type of Travel, 1997-2005 (%)

Travel Type	1997	1999	2001	2003	2005
FIT	47.6	51.2	56.6	52.2	39.9
Package	52.4	48.8	43.4	47.8	60.1
Total	**100.0**	**100.0**	**100.0**	**100.0**	**100.0**

Source: Analysis from KTO's raw data (2006)

2.6.7 Spending

Individual Korean outbound travellers' largest expense is airfare. Lodging, food and transportation are other major expenses. Types of expenses by outbound Korean travellers are listed below, for the years 1997 to 2005.

Spending by Individual Travellers to Foreign Countries, 1997-2005 (US$)

Spending by Travellers	1997	1999	2001	2003	2005
Total Cost	1,687	1,646	1,914	1,709	1,779
Airfare	604	698	792	773	794
Lodging	421	412	554	417	363
Food	224	259	283	233	222
Transportation	19	184	201	16	145
Culture	–	–	–	–	67
Sports	–	–	–	–	185
Amusement	176	175	268	19	139
Shopping	229	22	333	228	266
Others	257	26	253	152	88

Source: Analysis from KTO's raw data (2006)

Korean outbound group travellers spend most on travel package fee. Before 2005 other types of expenses were not yet reported in detail. The figures below show the type of spending by group traveller from 1997 to 2005. The biggest expense by Korean outbound group travellers goes to shopping, followed by transport, sports, amusement and culture. Spending has slightly increased since 2001.

Spending by Group Travellers, 1997-2005 (US$)

Spending by Travellers	1997	1999	2001	2003	2005
Total Costs	1,477	1,799	1,444	1,537	1,530
Package Fee	–	1,195	1,081	1,110	1,110
Food	–	–	–	–	64
Transport	–	–	–	–	123
Culture	–	–	–	–	79
Sports	–	–	–	–	102

Spending by Travellers	1997	1999	2001	2003	2005
Amusement	–	–	156	150	79
Shopping	–	–	264	268	340
Other	–	738	186	174	174

Source: Analysis from KTO's raw data (2006)

2.6.8 Shopping

Koreans generally spend money on shopping while they are abroad. The proportion of non-shoppers, however, has increased slightly. This could be due to a number of reasons. The availability of certain goods domestically may influence the choice to shop while abroad as might the purpose of visit, frequency of visit and the choice to travel individually or with a group.

Shopping	1997 (%)	1999 (%)	2001 (%)	2003 (%)	2005 (%)
Yes	98.0	96.0	93.6	88.7	92.8
No	2.0	4.0	6.4	11.3	7.2
Total	100.0	100.0	100.0	100.0	100.0

Source: Analysis from KTO's raw data (2006)

2.6.9 Shopping Venue

The majority of Korean outbound tourists choose to shop in duty-free shops. In 2005 almost 82% of travellers reported shopping in duty free shops. Other major shopping outlet types include general shops and stores as well as souvenir shops. The proportion of types of shopping outlet favored by Korean outbound tourists, are found in the following figures. Korean outbound tourists are quality consumers, purchasing well-known brands of cognac, whisky, cosmetics, leather goods, etc in duty-free shops, which are considered more reliable while shopping in foreign countries.

Shopping Venue, 1997-2005 (%)

Shopping Outlet Type	1997	1999	2001	2003	2005
Duty-free Shop	77.6	74.3	59.0	65.6	81.8
General Shop/Store	44.1	42.3	46.8	50.7	55.7
Souvenir Shop	38.2	33.6	34.0	38.2	45.6
Department Store	26.4	18.8	17.8	14.4	6.8
In-flight	–	–	0.7	1.4	1.0
Other	6.1	7.9	0.3	0.4	0.5

Source: Analysis from KTO's raw data (2006)

As shown in the above table, department stores are becoming a less popular shopping venue, mainly due to the language barriers. On the contrary, the use of general shops/stores and souvenir shops have been steadily increasing. These trends are mainly related to the increase interest in local culture. In-flight shopping is also becoming a new shopping outlet.

In conclusion, in order to sell more goods to Korean outbound travellers, PR activities including advertisement and dissemination of promotional materials should be taken strategically into account.

2.7 Travel Trade

This section provides an overview of the structure, size and type of administrative governance of the travel trade of the Republic of Korea. The tourism industry comprises of thousands of businesses, ranging across several sectors, from transport, tour companies and accommodation to visitor attractions. Each of these sectors offers a variety of products that can be enhanced through improved distribution; this is commonly achieved through intermediaries who package several different components.

Tourism enterprises operate in a global marketplace but, for a large majority, remain actors at the local level. The increased international tourism competition is forcing all businesses to look at innovative ways to improve the quality and market orientation of their products, their profitability and competitiveness. This new situation has forced the government to realize that tourism cannot grow on its own without some leadership and guidance, notably for the medium to long term. This increasingly competitive and global environment confronts the tourism industry with a wide range of challenges. The new market dynamics call also for more cooperation (e.g., on horizontal and vertical integration or diagonal integration, e-business models, or on human resource skills and competences), amongst tourism stakeholders.

Changes in the paradigm of cooperation and organization brought about changes in the national governmental administration. Changes influenced the decision to shift towards a development strategy for a balanced national and local government system that is decentralized. Support for the emergence of local public enterprises and local tourism organizations, an increase in local tourism development, changes in financial operations and greater diversity in society, are some of the noteworthy results. Through this decentralization effort, independent local development strategies have emerged.

The Ministry of Culture and Tourism (www.mct.go.kr) is one of the most important central government agencies of the Republic of Korea. The Ministry is responsible for affairs related to culture, arts, religion, tourism, and sports, and the organizational chart of the Ministry of Culture and Tourism can be found below.

Organizational Chart of the Ministry of Culture and Tourism of the Republic of Korea

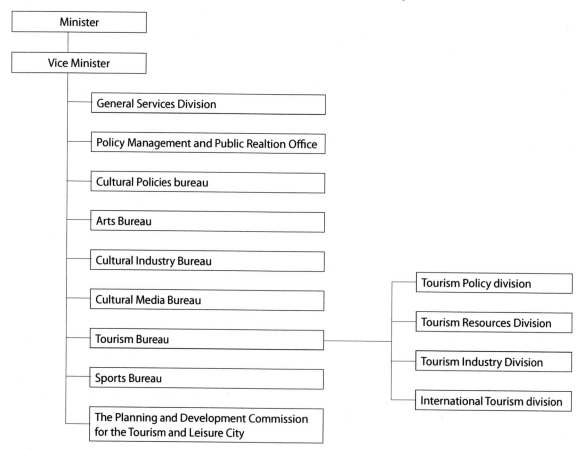

Source: Ministry of Culture and Tourism

The Tourism Bureau establishes and carries out policies to increase the number of foreign tourists, seeks to expand sightseeing opportunities for Koreans, and to promote tourism industry generally for both the local and international interests in the age of globalization.

The Korea Tourism Organization (ex-KNTO: http://www.knto.or.kr http://www.knto.or.kr) was established under the promulgation of the International Tourism Organization Law on June 26, 1962. The KTO's main objectives are: 1) to promote the Korean tourism industry, 2) to develop resources on Korean tourism, 3) to conduct training programs for human resources in tourism.

KTO has established 26 overseas offices to increase the number of foreign visitors interested in the Republic of Korea through various promotional activities. KTO also strives to create a better and more convenient environment for visitors. Furthermore, KTO makes an effort to provide healthy leisure activities and services for the residents of the Republic of Korea.

KTO's Organizational Chart

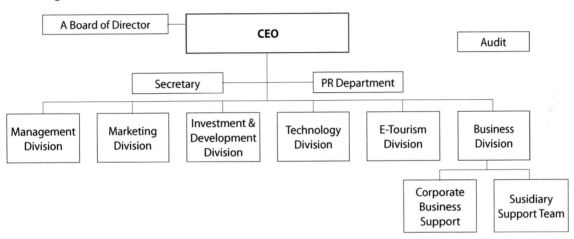

Source: Korea Tourism Organization

Korea Tourism Association and Korea Association of Travel Agents have overall responsibility for managing and supporting the tourism industry. The organization, functions and date of establishment are summarized below.

Major Travel Trade Associations in the Republic of Korea

Organization	Functions
Korea Tourism Association (established in March 1963)	• Representing tourism enterprises and coordinating the industry. • Promoting the tourism industry through co-operation with domestic and foreign organizations. • Promoting the interests and well-being of its members.
Korea Association of Travel Agents (established in December 1991)	• Promoting the interests of employees in the Republic of Korea's travel industry. • Being responsible for the collection and publication of travel research and statistics.

Source: Korea Tourism Association and Korea Association of Travel Agents (2005)

Travel agencies in the Republic of Korea are classified as general, overseas or domestic agencies. Since opening the industry to international partnerships in January 1991, the government has been striving to make the Korean tourism industry more competitive by taking measures to improve the management of its travel agencies, and by fostering competent professionals for the industry. As of December 2005 there were 9,521 travel agencies registered nationwide. There are 784 general travel agencies, 4,392 overseas travel agencies and 3,805 domestic travel agencies. The location and classification of travel agencies in the Republic of Korea are summarized below.

Location and Classification of Travel Agencies in the Republic of Korea, 2005

Location	Travel Agency Classification			
	Overseas	Domestic	General	Total
Seoul	2,651	1,068	606	4,325
Busan	389	308	33	730
Daegu	181	179	4	364
Incheon	78	80	7	165
Gwangju	123	121	10	254
Daejeon	168	164	3	335
Ulsan	44	49	3	96
Gyeonggi	416	506	31	953
Gangwon	97	124	14	235
Chungbuk	82	108	10	200
Chungnam	101	159	2	262
Jeonbuk	145	166	4	315
Jeonnam	114	186	6	306
Gyeongbuk	111	144	7	262
Gyeongnam	186	249	7	442
Jeju	46	194	37	277
Total	**4,932**	**3,805**	**784**	**9,521**

Source: Korea Tourism Association (2005)

2.8 Airlines

As of May 2005, the airline industry in the Republic of Korea has established cooperative agreements with 83 countries, 25 of which are Asian countries. The two major regular carriers of the Republic of Korea are Korean Air and Asiana Airlines. These two companies combined, offer services for 153 international routes. 497 flights covering 71 routes are to East Asian destinations and 210 flights covering 28 routes are to Southeast Asia.

Korean Air, with a fleet of 116 aircrafts, is one of the world's top 20 airlines, and operates almost 400 passenger flights per day to 91 cities in 31 countries. It is a founding member of SkyTeam, the global airlines alliance – partnering with Aero Mexico, Air France, Alitalia, CSA Czech Airlines, Continental Airlines, Delta Air Lines, KLM and Northwest Airlines – to provide customers with extensive worldwide destinations, flights and services. More information on Korean Air's programs, routes, frequency and partnerships is available at www.koreanair.com. Asiana Airlines, Inc, with a fleet of 58 aircraft operates 64 passenger flights per day to 54 cities in 17 counties. Cargo flights operated include destinations in 14 countries and 19 cities consisting of 16 routes. International air service by the Republic of Korea's two major airlines is listed below, and the following table summarizes the Republic of Korea's international airline industry's cooperative agreements. International air routes of the Republic of Korea's domestic carriers are also found thereafter.

International Air Service by the Republic of Korea's Two Major Airlines, 2006

Region	Number of Routes	Number of Air Service/Week	Passenger/Flight (Once a Week)
N/E Asia (China, Japan)	70	496 (KAL 265, AAR 231)	474/23
S/E Asia	28	210 (KAL 126, AAR 84)	174/36
Europe	19	75 (KAL 60, AAR 15)	40/35
Americas	32	151 (KAL 108, AAR 43)	105/43
Others	13	44 (KAL 31, AAR 13)	41/3
Total	162	976 (KAL 590, AAR 386)	834/140
Grand Total	33 countries, 96 cities, 162 routs, 955 flights/week		

Source: Ministry of Construction and Transportation (2006)

International Airline Industry Cooperative Agreements, 2006

Region	Bi-lateral	Unilateral
Asia (25 locations)	China, Thailand, Japan, Brunei, India, Mongolia, Vietnam, Malaysia, Hong Kong, Philippines, Singapore, Uzbekistan, Macao, Indonesia, Pakistan, Kazakhstan, Kyrgyzstan, Nepal, Cambodia, Azerbaijan, Taiwan, Province of China	Myanmar, Bangladesh, Maldives, Sri Lanka
Europe (26 locations)	UK, Poland, Russia, Czech, Yugoslavia, Romania, Malta, Bulgaria, Finland, Netherlands, Germany, Sweden, Denmark, Norway, Belgium, Switzerland, Ukraine, Austria, Portugal, Luxembourg, Iceland	France, Greece, Spain, Hungary, Italy
Americas (8 locations)	USA, Chile, Brazil, Argentina, Canada, Mexico, Peru	Panama
Africa (10 locations)	Tunisia, Sudan, Republic of South Africa, Morocco, Egypt	Liberia, Djibouti, Kenya, Gabon, Nigeria
Middle East (11 locations)	United Arab Emirates, Bahrain, Oman, Iran	Saudi Arabia, Jordan, Turkey, Kuwait, Iraq, Israel, Qatar
Oceania (3 locations)	Australia, New Zealand, Fiji	
Total (83 locations)	Bi-lateral total: 61 destinations	Unilateral Total: 22 destinations

Source: Ministry of Construction and Transportation (2006)

International Air Routes Serviced by the Republic of Korea's Two Major Domestic Carriers, 2006

Domestic Carriers	Number of Countries	Number of Cities	Number of Routes	Number of Flights/Week		
				Total	Passenger	Freight
Korean Air Lines	31	71	109	572	477	95
Asiana	21	57	84	383	350	31
Total	33	96	162	955	827	126

Source: Ministry of Construction and Transportation (2006)

2.9 Visa

Passengers must hold a valid passport and check for arrival documents at the country of destination or transit.

Visa Requirement, 2006

Section	Contents
When visas for country of destination or transit is not required.	• Traveling to countries with visa exemption agreements • Countries with visa exemption agreements for Korean citizens • When country of destination or transit requires reentry authorization • When country of destination or transit requires arrival visas.
Other notes	• When holding residential passports • Those with military duties or current soldiers • Dual citizens, first-time immigrants and foreign adoptee • Accompanying children on passport.

Source: Incheon International Airport Report(2006)

Visa Exemption

Section	Data
Destinations requiring a visa	Taiwan Province of China, Russian Federation, Myanmar, Bangladesh, Vietnam, Sri Lanka, Indonesia, India, China, Australia
Destinations not requiring a visa	• Guam, Singapore (during 14 days) • Macao (during 20 days) • The Philippines (during 21 days) • Hong Kong (during 30 days) • Thailand, Malaysia, New Zealand (during 90 days) • Japan

Source: Incheon International Airport Report (2006)

2.10 Observations

Observations from Korean outbound travellers are provided in this study. This information is critical when evaluating the outbound market as it can influence tourism packages and promotion when targeting the Korean outbound market and the region. Koreans generally report satisfaction with the accommodations available when traveling, and those who are dissatisfied have decreased over the past five years.

To a lesser extent, Koreans are satisfied with the food and dining available while abroad. It is worth mentioning that generally, Koreans have a strong preference for their own cuisine and are not enthusiastic about trying something too foreign, or 'local'. At least half of the Koreans traveling abroad reported satisfaction with the available shopping products as well as with the tour guides and services available. This indicates that as the popularity and influence of travel agencies and package tours increases, a certain amount of effort should be spent to ensure that the quality of tour guides and services increase accordingly. This is critical if market trends are to be sustainable in the coming years.

However, on a positive note, very few travellers reported dissatisfaction with the available tour programs, itineraries and their price. Equally, Koreans reported encountering fewer inconveniences during their travel abroad, especially regarding language, food and information.

The increase of package tours and pleasure travel for Koreans indicates changes in demographics as well as an increasing knowledge of travel choices. Destinations in the Asian region should respond to these trends with increasing sensitivity to the quality of all aspects of the travel product offered. This is particularly important if the destination intends to attract return visits. Since 1997, the number of Korean travellers indicating an intention to revisit has decreased dramatically. This would indicate that Koreans are more informed about destinations and therefore more competitions occur amongst destinations. Japan is the destination that most Koreans desire to visit and other destinations such as the United States of America and Australia have fallen in popularity. Following the trend of increasing travel information (thanks to travel agency advertising and the internet), Koreans are becoming less interested in traditional travel destinations while with the proper packaging and promotion, this could be a positive opportunity for previously less well known regional destinations, such as Vietnam, Indonesia and India to market themselves to the Korean outbound travellers.

Chapter 3

Outbound Traffic to Asia–Pacific Destinations

3.1 Existing Traffic

In this section, a general overview of available market intelligence from major Asian destinations is provided. Such intelligence includes airlines operating to destinations, tour operators and agents and programs, booking patterns, package/FITs, and general demographic composition of the traveller in terms of age, gender, and social status.

This market intelligence has been analyzed from raw data obtained from the Korean Tourism Organization's (KTO) Annual Survey on Korean Overseas Travel.

Moreover, this section focuses on existing and future trends which have been obtained from stakeholders' interviews (25 samples of tour operators, travel agents and airlines) so as to illustrate certain qualitative information in terms of accessibility, formalities, accommodation, local transport, guides, health, medical and insurance facilities, food and security, telecommunication, recreation and entertainment, information through NTOs, Internet, and services rendered by local agents.

Some of the general characteristics and findings are worthwhile to comment on, while the general profile for each destination is offered in the following sub-sections, including tables and graphs to illustrate their general characteristics.

As discussed in the previous section, Japan is the favorite destination for Koreans reporting a desire to visit a foreign country. In numbers, more Koreans visit Japan than any other destinations except China (about 19% of the outbound market). There are slightly more males than females, and the reported purpose for visiting is for pleasure, followed by business and visiting friends and relatives. Most travellers are employed in the private sector (probably male) or are unemployed (probably wives accompanying). Honeymoon, school excursions and other incentive tour programs attract Korean travellers from every age bracket, indicating that Japan is a mature and well-developed destination for the Korean outbound market. Koreans' decision to visit Japan is largely affected by the recommendations of friends and relatives, or by business considerations. They rely on the experiences of familiar others to inform them regarding their travel choices, but the internet is quickly becoming a major information source. Travel agencies converting their operations to e-business can capitalize on this trend by offering information and travel products.

Twice as many Koreans travel for leisure than for business. The main reason for pleasure travel to Japan is for sightseeing activities or shopping. Package travel and independent travel are equally chosen and independent travel is usually for business. Most visitors to Japan engage in shopping, preferring duty free shops and other stores rather than gift shops. They buy cosmetics, alcoholic beverages and souvenirs that are unique to Japan and suitable as gifts. Most travellers are satisfied with their visit in all sectors, but the language barrier is most commonly reported as inconvenience.

China is the most favorite travel destination, enjoying a growing market share over Japan. In 2005, almost 35% of the Republic of Korea's outbound market chose destinations in China. 65% of travellers were male, visiting for pleasure rather than for business.

Travellers are employed in the private sector and are in their forties. There is a wide variety of activities available for tourists. The travel decision is largely influenced by the recommendations of friends and relatives who are recognized as people with overseas experience. Travel agencies and the internet are enjoying a greater role as a source of travel information for China.

At least half of all those visiting China report leisure as the major purpose of travel, but business is also significant. For pleasure travellers, trips to China were not considered to be any more expensive than a similar domestic trip. Travellers reported having enjoyed city sightseeing, shopping and the natural scenery. There was an almost equal number of independent and package travel while business travel being the most frequently reported type of independent travel. Most visitors to China have enjoyed some shopping at stores or duty free shops and gift shops were also frequently visited. Korean travellers bought souvenirs more than alcoholic beverages or food because they were considered inexpensive and suitable as gifts.

Visitors to China were generally satisfied although there was some dissatisfaction reported regarding Chinese local food and the cleanliness of the accommodations. The language barrier has also been considered a major inconvenience while traveling. Nevertheless a large proportion of travellers reported no inconvenience was experienced.

Thailand is the third most popular regional destination for the Korean outbound market. About 7% of Korean outbound travellers visited Thailand in 2005. An almost equal number of male and female Koreans visit Thailand for pleasure. Visitors are unemployed or employed in the private sector and are usually in their twenties or thirties. Thailand is perceived as a very safe destination with a wide variety of activities available for tourists. From this profile it is apparent that Thailand is a major destination for the Republic of Korea's important outbound honeymoon travel market. Honeymooners visit Bangkok, Pattaya and Phuket. Price is a major influence for travel decisions, and information concerning the destination is generally obtained from people with overseas travel experience. Koreans who traveled to Thailand for pleasure indicated that they perceived no major difference in pricing when compared with a similar domestic trip. Visitors enjoy all forms of sightseeing and shopping. There are slightly more business independent travellers than package travel type. In Thailand, Koreans shop at stores, duty free shops and gift shops and purchase souvenirs because they are inexpensive and because they prefer those foreign products as gifts. Travellers to Thailand are generally satisfied with their visit although the taste of local Thai food and some unclean accommodations are key points that can cause dissatisfaction amongst them. The language barrier and food are also major inconveniences. Nevertheless, a large portion of travellers has reported no major inconveniences.

The Philippines is a destination that is only about half as popular as Thailand, with only a 5% share of the Korean outbound market. Koreans are six times more likely to visit China than the Philippines. As with other regional destinations, there are slightly more male than female travellers and they travel for pleasure. Korean travellers are unemployed or employed in the private sector and are in their twenties. The abundance of luxury hotels and exclusive resorts, fresh seafood and entertainment draw honeymooners to Manila and Cebu. Thailand and the Philippines compete for the Republic of Korea's honeymoon travel market via package travel advertising, while the recommendations of friends and relatives are not influential in comparison to other markets. This indicates that price and the availability of travel packages via travel agencies and the internet make the Philippines a small but potentially growing travel destination choice. People travel to the Philippines for business or pleasure, because it is a place they want to visit that is not more expensive than a similar domestic trip. Visitors enjoy natural scenery and city sightseeing as well as shopping. Package travel is more frequent than independent travel. Koreans shop at duty free shops for cosmetics and alcoholic beverages indicating that the local businesses do not promote their own handicrafts and other local products in their duty free shops in the Philippines. Koreans are traveling to the Philippines but are bringing back the standard gifts they purchase at duty free shops that are generally the same at any destination. Visitors to the Philippines are generally satisfied with their trips, only reporting the language barrier as an inconvenience. This could indicate that resorts in the Philippines maintain a high standard of service quality.

Hong Kong is a traditional regional destination that has enjoyed some marginal growth since 2003. Almost twice as many Korean outbound travellers reported pleasure rather than business as their main purpose of visit. They are employed in the private sector or unemployed and are in their 30s. Hong Kong Disneyland and shopping are the major attractions and the recommendations of friends and relatives are the most important influence in this case when making their travel choice when going to Hong Kong because it is perceived as a destination that is not significantly more expensive than a similar domestic trip. Visitors enjoy city sightseeing and shopping. They are independent travellers who purchase cosmetics as well as alcoholic beverages and clothing primarily at duty free shops. As with shopping decisions at other destinations, foreign products are preferred as gifts for friends and relatives back home in the Republic of Korea. Travellers generally reported satisfaction with their trips and no major inconveniences have been reported. Nevertheless, the language barrier was considered an inconvenience while visiting Hong Kong.

Australia is a less frequently visited but a stable destination for Koreans. There are slightly more females than males visiting Australia, they primarily visit for pleasure rather than business and they are unemployed and in their 20s. Australia is popular for its natural resources and rural tourism as well as other leisure sports tours. Unlike the Republic of Korea's major regional destinations, this destination selection is largely influenced by package travel advertisement and destination image, and the major information sources are from travel agencies and the internet. Koreans travel to Australia for pleasure because it is a place they want to visit. They enjoy hot springs and other natural scenery as well as shopping in the form of package travel. They shop in duty free shops for cosmetics as gifts or because there is no similar product in the Republic of Korea. Quality is also a key reason for shopping. Generally, visitors to Australia reported satisfaction with their trips while the language barrier was considered an inconvenience.

Indonesia is a minor regional travel destination for Koreans, but has enjoyed a slight but steady growth recently. More males than females travel to Indonesia, but the gap has been closing over the past five years. Pleasure is the main reason for travel, and visitors are almost equally employed in the private sector or unemployed, and are in their 30s. Indonesia is home to key honeymoon destinations such as Bali and Bintan, and Jakarta city tours are popular as well. Package travel advertisement influence the travel decision, and travel agencies are the key source of travel information. People travel to Indonesia for honeymoons and to enjoy the natural scenery, shopping and the nightlife or entertainment. They shop in duty free shops for souvenirs and alcoholic beverages. Preference for foreign products as gifts and the cheaper price influence the purchasing decision. Travellers reported neither satisfaction nor dissatisfaction with their trips to Indonesia, and the major inconvenience encountered was cash exchange. Indonesia could probably benefit as a destination, with better tourism infrastructure and information.

A peripheral market for the Republic of Korea outbound tourism is India. Only 35,508 Koreans visited this destination in 2005. Most were male, traveling for pleasure or for business, employed in the private sector and in their forties. A variety of factors influence the travel decision and information on India, but the internet is a key source. The key purpose of travel is for business or pleasure and most Koreans reported India as a place they had wanted to visit. Natural scenery and city sightseeing as well as shopping were the major activities enjoyed by Koreans, the majority of them was independent travellers. Those who engaged in shopping did so at various stores and purchased souvenirs as well as a broad variety of other items. Travellers indicated the language barrier as a inconvenience. India is a small market for the Koreans, but offers a great variety of activities which is positive for the potential growth of India for the outbound travellers of the Republic of Korea.

In general, the Korean outbound market is fairly homogeneous. There are slightly more males than females outbound travellers and they are employed in the private sector or unemployed (mainly housewives and students). They travel as couples or as families for pleasure. The Republic of Korea's outbound honeymoon market is particularly visible in destinations such as Japan, Thailand and the Philippines. Their travel decisions are largely influenced by recommendations of friends and relatives but the role of travel agencies and the internet for providing travel information has grown significantly. Price and quality are major factors influencing the travel decision and Korean tourists are particularly sensitive to the quality and availability of particular food and accommodations. The major travel inconvenience for Koreans is the language barrier and this could be partially relieved with the availability of better travel information. Korean travellers enjoy sightseeing in general but are not particularly resourceful shoppers. They prefer the convenience of duty free shops and enjoy buying things that are of a type and quality that might not be available back in their country. These goods are usually bought for gifts to others.

3.1.1 Australia

Existing traffic and traffic patterns

Australia is a destination that is less frequently visited in the Asia-Pacific region by Korean outbound travellers. 198,088 Koreans visited Australia in 2005. Although Australia is becoming a favorable destination, two factors, high price and distance, are the main constraints for Koreans. The table below indicates the total numbers, percentage change and percentage share of Korean departures by gender to Australia from 2001 to 2005. More Korean females (51.3%) visited Australia .

Korean Departures by Gender to Australia, 2001-2005

Year	Total		Male			Female		
	Number	+/- (%)	Number	+/- (%)	Share (%)	Number	+/- (%)	Share (%)
2001	148,402	12.1	73,795	7.8	49.7	74,607	16.7	50.3
2002	160,867	8.4	78,441	6.3	48.8	82,426	10.5	51.2
2003	172,555	7.3	85,664	9.2	49.6	86,891	5.4	50.4
2004	172,265	-0.2	84,783	-1.0	49.2	87,482	0.7	50.8
2005	198,088	15.0	96,363	13.7	48.7	101,725	16.3	51.3

Source: Analysis from KTO's raw data (2006)

Koreans visit Australia for pleasure rather than business. As Korean immigration to Australia has increased recently, visiting friends and relatives (VFR) has increased accordingly. As indicated in the table below, 16.1% Korean travellers to Australia indicated pleasure as the main purpose of their visit in 2005. Due to active promotion activities in the Republic of Korea by Australian tourism organizations, pleasure trips will be steadily increasing in the future.

Growth of Korean Departures by Purpose to Australia, 2001-2005

Category	2001		2002		2003		2004		2005	
	Number	+/- (%)	Number	+/- (%)	Number	+/- (%)	Number	+/- (%)	Number	+/- (%)
Pleasure	95,533	17.7	109,625	14.8	116,337	6.1	116,611	0.2	135,389	16.1
Business	14,473	1.1	12,194	-15.7	12,371	1.5	12,246	-1.0	12,128	-1.0
VFR*	15,860	-9.2	14,931	-5.9	16,804	12.5	16,133	-4.0	19,930	23.5
Official	484	-5.3	444	-8.3	499	12.4	490	-1.8	445	-9.2
Convention	2,914	51.7	1,434	-50.8	1,704	-18.8	1,484	-12.9	1,435	-3.3
Others	19,138	12.5	22,239	16.2	24,840	11.7	25,301	1.9	28,761	13.7

* Excluding crew members
Source: Analysis from KTO's raw data (2006)

Most visitors to Australia are unemployed (it is assumed that this segment is mostly housewives and retired people), but students and educators are also large demographic segments of the Republic of Korea's outbound tourist market to that country. The following table illustrates the details of Korean departures by occupation to Australia from 2001 to 2005. Young Korean students prefer Australia for pursuing English language courses.

Growth of Korean Departures by Occupation to Australia, 2001-2005

Category	2001		2002		2003		2004		2005	
	Number	+/- (%)	Number	+/- (%)	Number	+/- (%)	Number	+/- (%)	Number	+/- (%)
Official	2,510	41.7	2,939	17.1	4,498	53.0	4,209	-6,4	4,432	5.3
Private Sector	–	–	44,297	–	48,667	9.9	45,792	-5.9	47,455	3.6
Self-Employed	7,409	35.5	6,129	-17.3	5,807	-5.3	5,106	-12.1	5,563	9.0
Educator	–	–	5,285	–	5,901	11.7	5,898	-0.1	6,295	6.7
Student	–	–	31,571	–	35,671	13.0	38,585	8.2	47,258	22,5
Others	–	–	10,962	–	10,938	-0.2	10,704	-2.1	11.301	5.6
Unemployed	–	–	63,414	–	65,031	2.6	65,846	1.3	79.817	21.2

Source: Analysis from KTO's raw data (2006)

Most travellers to Australia are in their 20s (63,521 for the year 2005) and in their 50s or more. The detailed breakdown of Korean departures by age to Australia is contained in the following table for the years 2001 to 2005.

Growth of Korean Departures by Age to Australia, 2001-2005

Category	2001		2002		2003		2004		2005	
	Number	+/- (%)	Number	+/- (%)	Number	+/- (%)	Number	+/- (%)	Number	+/- (%)
0 – 20	22,068	12.9	23,405	6.1	25,947	10.9	26,736	3.0	29,208	9.3
21 – 30	42,714	11.0	45,657	6.9	50,417	10.4	50,043	-0.7	63,521	26.9
31 – 40	33,489	16.3	33,848	1.1	37,046	9.5	37,462	1.1	40,692	8.6
41 – 50	25,098	17.1	27,378	9.1	30,192	10.3	30,448	0.8	32,184	5.7
51 – 60	17,484	4.4	20,367	16.5	20,320	-0.2	19,659	-3.3	22,848	16.2
> 61	10,780	3.1	13,942	29.3	12,591	-9.7	11,792	-6.3	13,668	15.9

Source: KTO

The following data was obtained from interviews with tour operators, travel agencies and airlines, and Korean representative of Tourism Australia as well as related websites.

Evaluation of Existing Traffic and Traffic Patterns in Australia

Category	Contents
Ease of entry	• ETA Visa (Electronic Visitor Visa) is required
Accommodation	• Variety levels of hotels • Camping, youth hostel. B&B (Bed and Breakfast)
Local transportation	• Convenient transportation system • Domestic flight, city rail, ferry, coach,
Health, medical and insurance facilities	• Excellent medical center • High quality of welfare system

Category	Contents		
Security	• Most of the cities are safe		
Food	• Popular for seafood, wine, organic and dairy produces		
Telecommunications	• Offer the latest telecommunication		
Recreation and Entertainment	• Opera, concert, musical		
	• Many shopping center		
	• National park, rainforest, outback tour,		
	• Sunbathing, swimming, snorkeling, fishing, yacht tour		
Tour products	• Beach and coral tour, Gold Coast tour		
	• City tour, shopping, Perth city tour		
	• Farm stay(a sheep ranch, a farm, a winery),		
	• National park, rainforest, outback tour,		
	• Sunbathing, swimming, snorkeling,		
	• Fishing, yacht tour		
Flight Schedule	**Route**	**Korean Airline**	**Asiana Airline**
	Incheon – Sydney	7 flights/week	7 flights/week
	Incheon – Brisbane	3 flights/week	–

Source: Korean Airline, Asiana Airline, Tourism Australia, Embassy of Australia

Factors affecting destination selection

For Koreans, major information sources influencing the decision to travel to Australia include the recommendations of friends or relatives, package travel advertisement, and/or favorable image of Australian destinations. Korean travellers to Australia reported travel agencies and people with overseas travel experiences as their major sources for travel information. All major factors affecting the travel decision are listed in the table below. The sources of travel information are listed in the subsequent table.

Factors Affecting Destination Selection (%)

Package Travel advertisement by Travel Agency	23.6
NTO Promotion	1.1
Friends/Relatives Recommendation	28.1
Internet Search	15.7
A favorable destination image	20.2
Mass Media	1.1
Price	2.3
Business	7.9

Source: Analysis from KTO's raw data (2006)

Travel Information Sources (%)

Travel Agency	33.7
People with Overseas Travel Experiences	30.3
Guidebooks	3.4
Internet	32.6

Source: Analysis from KTO's raw data (2006)

Purpose of travel

Outbound tourists bound for Australia reported their purpose for visiting as leisure and/or relaxation. In the following table, respondents' first and second response to a multiple response survey indicates that leisure and relaxation are the main purpose for most Korean visitors to Australia. Honeymoon, education and training in Australia are becoming a big market segment of the Republic of Korea.

The Purpose of Travel (%)

	1st Choice	2nd Choice
Leisure/Relaxation	66.2	33.7
VFR	10.1	1.1
Business	3.4	3.4
Convention	3.4	1.1
Education and Training	3.4	39.3
Culture/Sports	3.4	–
Honeymoon	10.1	–

Source: Analysis from KTO's raw data (2006)

The following table details the main reasons for traveling to Australia. Pleasure travellers to Australia reported engaging in a number of activities including the enjoyment of natural scenery and historic monuments.

The Main Reason of Travel (%)

	1st Choice	2nd Choice
There is no difference in travel cost, compared to domestic travel	21.3	5.6
I have visited almost all destinations in Republic of Korea	1.1	9.0
A place that I want to visit	43.8	23.6
Sense of satisfaction with overseas travel	23.6	9.0
Having opportunities for group travel	5.6	38.2
Others	4.6	1.1

Source: Analysis from KTO's raw data (2006)

The 11 most frequently indicated activities are also listed below:

Activities for Pleasure Travellers to Australia (%)

Natural Scenery	20.5
Historic Monuments	8.6
Cultural Events/Festivals	7.8
Hot Springs	2.2
Nightlife/Entertainment	12.7
Swimming/Sunbathing	2.9
Hiking/Camping	2.2
Golf	1.0
Casino	1.2
City Sightseeing	21.0
Shopping	19.9

Source: Analysis from KTO's raw data (2006)

Package vs. FIT

Choices of travel type by outbound tourists to Australia are largely package travel type. There are fewer independent travellers as indicated in the table below. The specific type of travel to Australia for Koreans is for visiting friends and relatives or for business.

Package vs. FIT (%)

Independent Travel	20.2
Package Travel	79.8
Total	**100.0**

Source: Analysis from KTO's raw data (2006)

Satisfaction rate

Korean visitors to Australia generally reported satisfaction with their overall visit. Over 60% of visitors was at least somewhat satisfied. A very small number of respondents reported being dissatisfied. The main reason for dissatisfaction is caused by aggressive selling or dishonest travel guides.

Korean visitors to Australia reported various degrees of satisfaction and dissatisfaction depending upon the tourism sector. The degree of satisfaction or dissatisfaction by sector is detailed in the tables below: accommodation, food, shopping items, tour guide's service, tour itinerary and contents. Korean visitors to Australia generally have reported being satisfied with their experience in terms of all these sectors.

Satisfaction Level of by Sector (%)

Accommodation	Food	Shopping	Items	Guide Service	Tour Itinerary & Contents
Very satisfied	9.0	6.7	6.7	3.4	6.8
Somewhat satisfied	66.3	47.2	61.8	51.7	71.9
Neutral	14.6	33.8	23.7	18.0	16.9
Somewhat dissatisfied	–	10.1	1.1	11.2	2.2
Very dissatisfied	–	–	–	–	1.1
I don't know	10.1	2.2	6.7	15.7	1.1

Korean visitors to Australia indicated language barrier as the major travel inconvenience during their visit. Food followed as a distant second. Almost 33% of respondents indicated that they encountered no travel inconvenience. All 12 types of travel inconvenience are listed in the following table:

Travel Inconveniences (%)

Language Barrier	42.9
Travel Information	1.8
Information Desk Service	2.8
Local Transportation	2.8
Forced Employee Tips	3.7
Forced Selling	4.8
Nightlife/Entertainment	1.0
Food	10.5
Criminal/Safety	1.0
Forced the additional Travel Expenditure	3.8
Guide Tip	2.9
Airplane Transfer	1.0
Nothing	21.0
Total	**100.0**

Source: Analysis from KTO's raw data (2006)

3.1.2 China

Existing traffic and traffic patterns

Mainland China is a favorite destination in the Asia-Pacific region for Korean outbound travellers. 2,960,642 people from the Republic of Korea's outbound market visited China in 2005. The number of Korean visitors to China has increased remarkably. However, even though more female Koreans are traveling abroad, there are more Korean males visiting China. In 2005 almost 35% of the Republic of Korea's outbound market chose China as an outbound destination. 65% of travellers was male, visiting for pleasure rather than for business. This figure is related to golf tours organized by male groups.

Because green fees in the Republic of Korea are relatively expensive, Korean male golfers tend to enjoy 2 or 3 day golfing in China. The following table indicates the total numbers, percentage change and percentage share of Korean departures by gender to China from 2001 to 2005.

Korean Departures by Gender to China, 2001-2005

Year	Total		Male			Female		
	Number	+/- (%)	Number	+/- (%)	Share (%)	Number	+/- (%)	Share (%)
2001	1,297,746	25.6	879,234	23.8	67.8	418,512	29.5	32.2
2002	1,722,128	32.7	1,145,638	30.3	66.5	576,490	37.7	33.5
2003	1,569,245	-8.9	1,101,205	-3.9	70.2	468,040	-18.8	29.8
2004	2,334,781	48.8	1,573,908	42.9	67.4	760,873	62.6	32.6
2005	2,960,642	26.8	1,939,551	23.2	65.5	1,021,091	34.2	34.5

Source: Analysis from KTO's raw data (2006)

Since 2001, Koreans have consistently visited China for pleasure rather than business. As indicated in the table and figure below, 15.4% of travellers to China indicated pleasure as the main purpose of their visit. Significantly, visiting friends and relatives (VFR) has also increased, mainly due to the increase in temporary migrations from the Republic of Korea to China for working and establishment of businesses. The purpose of official visits has decreased by 7.5% in 2005, compared to the previous year.

Growth of Korean Departures by Purpose to China, 2001-2005

Category	2001		2002		2003		2004		2005	
	Number	+/- (%)	Number	+/- (%)	Number	+/- (%)	Number	+/- (%)	Number	+/- (%)
Pleasure	596,992	43.6	867,522	45.3	694,918	-19.9	1,191,691	71.5	1,637,569	37.4
Business	529,554	14.4	633,736	19.7	666,781	5.2	853,094	27.9	938,438	10.0
VFR*	88,394	-0.3	103,738	17.4	106,626	2.8	154,511	44.9	223,655	44.8
Official	4,492	80.8	3,779	-15.9	3,880	2.7	4,099	5.6	3,793	-7.5
Convention	9,803	2.5	8,624	-12.0	5,271	-38.9	9,726	84.5	10,858	11.6
Others	68,511	27.3	104,729	52.9	91,769	-12.4	121,660	32.6	146,329	20.3

* Excluding crew members
Source: Analysis from KTO's raw data (2006)

Most visitors to China are people employed in the education sector and this is followed closely by those who are unemployed, consisting mostly of housewives who are the fastest growing market of outbound tourists of the Republic of Korea. Groups of students visiting for historical sites inspections and Chinese language courses are a big segment among the Korean outbound market. The following table illustrates the details of Korean departures to China by occupation from 2001 to 2005.

Growth of Korean Departures by Occupation to China, 2001-2005

Category	2001		2002		2003		2004		2005	
	Number	+/- (%)	Number	+/- (%)	Number	+/- (%)	Number	+/- (%)	Number	+/- (%)
Official	12,475	84.7	16,200	29.9	13,855	-14.5	21,514	55.3	26,402	22.7
Private Sector	–	–	695,234	–	704,410	1.3	957,783	36.0	1,120,338	17.0
Self-Employed	206,591	16.3	234,331	13.4	224,851	-4.0	321,368	42.9	387,172	20.5
Educator	–	–	34,461	–	27,160	-21.2	47,084	73.4	60,990	29.5
Student	–	–	147,910	–	133,398	-9.8	213,239	59.9	291,729	36.8
Others	–	–	79,413	–	55,213	-30.5	83,289	50.9	98,520	18.3
Unemployed	–	–	523,753	–	417,684	-20.3	701,394	67.9	987,791	40.8

Source: Analysis from KTO's raw data (2006)

Most travellers to China are in their 40s (862,001 for the year 2005), followed closely by those in their thirties. The detailed breakdown of Korean departures by age to China is contained in the following table for the years 2001 to 2005:

GrowthKorean Departures by Age to China, 2001-2005

Category	2001		2002		2003		2004		2005	
	Number	+/- (%)	Number	+/- (%)	Number	+/- (%)	Number	+/- (%)	Number	+/- (%)
0 – 20	90,595	50.1	133,116	46.9	127,843	-4.0	201,338	57.5	286,591	42.3
21 – 30	152,862	18.1	198,097	29.6	178,070	-10.1	261,552	46.9	319,233	22.1
31 – 40	313,667	17.5	405,644	29.3	386,417	-4.7	529,511	37.0	625,643	18.2
41 – 50	368,460	27.6	499,527	35.6	486,244	-2.7	697,333	43.4	862,001	23.6
51 – 60	236,311	26.1	303,140	28.3	257,302	-15.1	413,017	60.5	549,687	33.1
> 61	142,447	35.3	191,778	34.6	140,695	-26.6	242,920	72.7	329,787	35.8

Source: Analysis from KTO's raw data (2006)

The following information was obtained from interviews with tour operators, travel agencies and airlines, and Korean representative of China National Tourism Administration as well as related websites.

Evaluation of Existing Traffic and Traffic Patterns in China

Category	Contents
Ease of entry	• Require a visa to enter China
Accommodation	• Variety of accommodation at all levels • Prices depend on the level of the hotel
Local transportation	• Bicycle is the most popular form of transportation • There are also trains, buses and taxis • Subways only available in Beijing and Shanghai
Health, medical and insurance facilities	• Medical industry is growing • Problem of public health in countryside and/or suburb

Category	Contents		
Security	• Big cities are seen as safe • Maintenance of public peace and order		
Food	• Good variety of food • Plenty of Western and Eastern food		
Telecommunications	• Developed Telecommunication industry • International calls, faxes, and internet can be used		
Recreation and entertainment	• Wide variety of activities available for tourists • Chinese opera (kyungguk)		
Tour products	• Mountain Tour • City tour to Beijing, Shanghai, Zhangjiajie • Shanghai Convention incentive tour		
Flight schedule	**Route**	**Korean Airline**	**Asiana Airline**
	Incheon – Beijing	10 flights/week	14 flights/week
	Incheon – Shanghai	15 flights/week	24 flights/week
	Incheon – Xiamen	3 flights/week	
	Incheon – Shenyang	18 flights/week	
	Incheon – Shenzhen	3 flights/week	5 flights/week
	Incheon – Sanya	2 flights/week	
	Incheon – Yanji	2 flights/week	2 flights/week
	Incheon – Urumqi	2 flights/week	
	Incheon – Wuhan	2 flights/week	4 flights/week
	Incheon – Ulaanbaatar	3 flights/week	
	Incheon – Weihai	2 flights/week	4 flights/week
	Incheon – Jinan	2 flights/week	5 flights/week
	Incheon – Qingdao	14 flights/week	7 flights/week
	Incheon – Kunming	2 flights/week	
	Incheon – Tianjin	12 flights/week	

Source: Korean Airline, Asiana Airline, Embassy of China in Korea, CNTO

Factors affecting destination selection

For Koreans, major source of influence affecting their decisions to travel to China include the recommendations of friends or relatives, business reasons, or packaged travel advertisement. More than 30% of Korean travellers to China reported the recommendation of friends or relatives as the major factor influencing their travel decision. Word of mouth is an important factor affecting Korean travel decision to China. Both NTO promotion and internet are not major factors, contrary to the general expectation. Another major factor is the business opportunity and trade that one may generate by visiting China. All major factors affecting the travel decision are listed in the following table

Factors Affecting Destination Selection (%)

Package Travel Ads	17.4
NTO Promotion	1.7
Friends/Relatives Recommendation	33.3
Internet	4.0
Destination Image	7.9
Mass Media	0.5
Prices	5.6
Business	29.6
Total	**100.0**

Source: Analysis from KTO's raw data (2006)

The purpose of travel

Outbound tourists bound for China reported their purpose of visit as leisure or relaxation. In the table below, respondents' first and second responses to a multiple response survey indicate that business is a second purpose for most Korean visitors to China.

Purpose of Travel (%)

	1st Choice	2nd Choice
Leisure/Relaxation	53.5	43.0
VFR	6.4	3.3
Business	32.2	0.3
Convention	2.2	0.2
Training	2.4	0.3
Culture/Sports Activities	2.1	0.6
Others	1.2	1.2

Source: Analysis from KTO's raw data (2006)

Main Reason of Travel (%)

	1st Choice	2nd Choice
There is no difference in travel cost, compared to domestic travel	30.2	11.5
I have visited almost all destinations in Republic of Korea	2.7	5.3
A place that I want to visit	34.4	24.7
Not many tourist attractions in Republic of Korea	2.7	5.2
Sense of satisfaction with overseas travel	17.0	27.9
Not many entertainment facilities in Republic of Korea	0.2	0.6
Having opportunities for group travel	6.4	4.6
Others	6.4	0.3

Source: Analysis from KTO's raw data (2006)

Package vs. FIT

Choices of travel type by outbound tourists to China are almost evenly divided between FITs (52.5%) and package travel (47.5%). There are slightly more independent travellers as indicated in the following table. The specific type of travel to China for Koreans is package travel, business, VFR or SMERF (Social, Military, Education, Religion, and Fraternity) groups.

Specific Type of Independent Travel or Package Travel (%)

VFR	18.4
Business	31.6
Backpacking	1.1
Official	1.4
Honeymoon	.2
Package Travel	23.7
SMERF Group	19.6
SMERF Independence	2.0
Training	2.0
Total	**100.0**

Source: Analysis from KTO's raw data (2006)

Satisfaction rate

Korean visitors to China are generally satisfied with their overall visit. Only a very small number of respondents reported being dissatisfied. The main reasons for being dissatisfied are indicated in the table below. They mostly are related to the difference in food taste and accommodation. Cleanliness is also one of the reasons for the dissatisfaction of the Korean visitors to China.

Reason for Being either Very Dissatisfied or Somewhat Dissatisfied (%)

Expensive transportation fee	2.4
Food doesn't taste well	21.9
Unkind restaurant employees	2.4
Dishonest tour guides	7.3
Coercion to provide tips	2.4
Unclean restaurants	7.3
Unclean accommodations	24.4
Inconvenient transportations	2.4
Poor street maintenance	2.4
Noise	2.4
Unclean streets	12.2
Dissatisfied with tour itinerary	4.9
Tight schedule of itinerary	2.4
Expensive price	2.4
Coercive shopping	2.8

Korean visitors to China reported various degrees of satisfaction and dissatisfaction depending upon the tourism sector. The degree of satisfaction or dissatisfaction by sector is detailed in the tables below: accommodation, food, shopping items, tour guide service, and tour itinerary. Korean visitors to China generally reported satisfaction with their overall experience.

Satisfaction Level by Sector (%)

	Accommodation	Food	Shopping Items	Guide Service	Tour Itinerary
Very satisfied	6.6	3.7	2.8	9.0	5.4
Somewhat satisfied	42.4	34.2	43.7	30.8	50.0
Neutral	33.8	36.8	34.6	18.0	34.8
Somewhat dissatisfied	6.6	19.2	5.3	4.2	3.2
Very dissatisfied	2.0	5.0	0.9	0.6	0.6
I don't know	8.6	1.1	12.7	37.4	6.0

Travel inconveniences

Korean visitors to China almost unanimously indicated language barrier as the major travel inconvenience encountered during their visit. Food was the second major travel inconvenience indicated. Almost 35% of the respondents indicated that they encountered no travel inconvenience. All 22 kinds of travel inconvenience are listed in the table below:

Travel Inconveniences (%)

Language Barrier	34.7
Money Exchange	1.2
Airplane Reservation	1.2
Tour Information	1.8
Information Desk Service	1.4
Local Transportation	7.7
Forced Employee Tips	0.9
Coercive Selling	3.1
Nightlife/Entertainment	0.7
Food	19.5
Criminal/Safety	2.8
Forced additional expenses to travel agency	0.1
Forced tips to guides	1.4
Airplane Transfer	0.3
Accommodation	0.7
Toilet	0.7
Unkind Employee at Airport	0.2
Price	0.1
Rip-off	0.2

Unkind Flight Crew	0.2
Entrance Processing	0.1
Nothing	21.0
Total	**100.0**

Source: Analysis from KTO's raw data (2006)

3.1.3 Hong Kong

Existing traffic and traffic patterns

Hong Kong is an important destination for Korean outbound travellers in the Asian region. 344,393 people visited Hong Kong in 2005. However, even though more female Koreans are traveling abroad, there are still more Korean males visiting Hong Kong. The following table indicates the total numbers, percentage change and percentage share of Korean departures by gender to Hong Kong from 2001 to 2005.

Korean Departures by Gender to Hong Kong, 2001-2005

Year	Total		Male			Female		
	Number	+/- (%)	Number	+/- (%)	Share (%)	Number	+/- (%)	Share (%)
2001	234,015	15.6	136,048	12.6	58.1	98,003	20.1	41.9
2002	253,692	8.4	145,797	7.2	57.5	107,895	10.1	42.5
2003	210,586	-17.0	122,570	-15.9	58.2	88,016	-18.4	41.8
2004	305,351	45	173,305	41.4	56.8	132,046	50.0	43.2
2005	344.393	12.8	194.841	12.4	56.6	149,552	13.3	43.4

Source: Analysis from KTO's raw data (2006)

Koreans have consistently visited Hong Kong for pleasure rather than for business since 2001. As indicated in the following table, 13.4% of travellers to Hong Kong indicated pleasure as the main purpose of their visit.

Growth of Korean Departures by Purpose to Hong Kong, 2001-2005

Category	2001		2002		2003		2004		2005	
	Number	+/- (%)	Number	+/- (%)	Number	+/- (%)	Number	+/- (%)	Number	+/- (%)
Pleasure	108,985	32.6	130,236	19.5	111,441	-14.4	173,233	55.5	196,469	13.4
Business	94,022	6.6	93,250	-0.8	75,076	-19.5	101,786	35.6	109,682	7.8
VFR*	17,793	-13.7	16,.057	-9.8	14,840	-7.6	18,632	25.6	25,512	36.9
Official	404	25.1	459	13.6	302	-34.2	452	49.7	402	-11.1
Convention	3,219	16.3	2,319	-28	1,286	-44.6	2,175	69.1	2,264	4.1
Others	9,628	15.0	11,371	18.1	7,641	-32.8	9,073	18.7	10,064	10.9

* Excluding crew members
Source: Analysis from KTO's raw data (2006)

Most visitors to Hong Kong are people employed in the private sector. Those who are unemployed (mostly housewives and retirees) also make up a large segment of the Republic of Korea's outbound tourist market to Hong Kong. The following table illustrates the details of Korean departures by occupation to Hong Kong from 2001 to 2005.

Growth of Korean Departures by Occupation to Hong Kong, 2001-2005

Category	2001		2002		2003		2004		2005	
	Number	+/- (%)	Number	+/- (%)	Number	+/- (%)	Number	+/- (%)	Number	+/- (%)
Official	1,528	26.9	2,020	32.2	1,797	-11.0	2,969	65.2	3,300	11.1
Private Sector	–	–	127,719	–	105,870	-17.1	152,892	44.4	166,361	8.8
Self-Employed	14,607	16.4	14,380	-1.6	10,369	-27.9	14,810	42.8	17,433	17.7
Educator	–	–	4,451	–	3,867	-13.1	5,681	46.9	6,849	20.6
Student	–	–	18,118	–	17,396	-4.0	23,213	33.4	26,444	13.9
Others	–	–	17,658	–	12,646	-28.4	16,947	34.0	18,521	9.3
Unemployed	–	–	75,664	–	63,304	-16.3	94,555	49.4	110,874	17.3

Source: Analysis from KTO's raw data (2006)

Most travellers to Hong Kong are in their thirties (109,423 for the year 2005), followed by those in their forties and twenties. The detailed breakdown of Korean departures by age to Hong Kong is contained in the table below, for the years 2001 to 2005:

Growth of Korean Departures by Age to Hong Kong, 2001-2005

Category	2001		2002		2003		2004		2005	
	Number	+/- (%)	Number	+/- (%)	Number	+/- (%)	Number	+/- (%)	Number	+/- (%)
0 – 20	17,330	30.6	18,646	7.6	17,956	-3.7	22,402	24.8	26,468	18.2
21 – 30	55,851	17.7	57,338	2.7	45,778	-20.2	73,238	60.0	79,820	9.0
31 – 40	74,560	13.3	81,447	9.2	66,390	-18.5	96,683	45.6	109,423	13.2
41 – 50	53,543	16.4	60,316	12.6	51,561	-14.5	71,368	38.4	81,254	13.9
51 – 60	26,412	11.7	28,333	7.3	22,533	-20.5	32,552	44.5	36,747	12.9
> 61	11,682	11.1	13,430	15.0	11,031	-17.9	14,824	34.4	16,070	8.4

Source: Analysis from KTO's raw data (2006)

The following information was obtained from interviews with tour operators, travel agencies and airlines, and Korean representative of Hong Kong Tourism Board (HKTB) as well as related websites:

Evaluation of Existing Traffic and Traffic Patterns in Hong Kong

Category	Contents
Ease of entry	• Visa free entry
Accommodation	• Wide variety of hotels • Many luxury hotels with suite rooms
Local transportation	• Convenient and efficient public transportation system • Airport Express Rail, bus, Star-ferry etc.

Health, medical and insurance facilities	• Excellent medical centers • High quality of welfare system		
Security	• Major buildings or tourist attractions have security		
Food	• Good variety of food • Abundant fresh seafood		
Telecommunications	• High standard • Roaming is not a problem		
Recreation and entertainment	• Shopping is popular • Wonderful night view		
Tourism products	• City tour, Express Tour etc. • Disneyland		
Flight schedule	Route	Korean Airline	Asiana Airline
	Incheon – Hong Kong	15 flights/week	14 flights/week

Source: Korean Airline, Asiana Airline, Hong Kong Tourism Board

Factors affecting destination selection

For Koreans, major information sources affecting the decision to travel to Hong Kong include the recommendations by friends or relatives, while travel for business reasons is equally important. More than 40% of Korean travellers to Hong Kong reported the recommendations of friends or relatives as the major factor affecting their travel. The major travel information source was from people with overseas travel experience. Factors affecting the travel decision, and travel information sources are listed in the tables below:

Factors Affecting Destination Selection (%)

Package Travel advertisement	4.5
Friends/Relatives Recommendation	45.3
Favorable Destination Image	4.5
Low Price	4.5
Business Related	41.2
Total	**100.0**

Source: Analysis from KTO's raw data (2006)

Travel Information Sources (%)

Travel Agency	18.1
People with Overseas Travel Experiences	40.8
Guidebooks	4.5
Internet	27.6
Company	4.5
Others	4.5

Source: Analysis from KTO's raw data (2006)

The Purpose of travel

Outbound tourists to Hong Kong reported their purpose of visit as leisure or relaxation (65.3%). In the table below, respondents' responses to a survey indicate that business is a second purpose for most Korean visitors to Hong Kong, followed by visiting friends and relatives (VFR).

The Purpose of Travel (%)

Leisure/Relaxation	65.3
Business	31.6
VFR	3.1

Source: Analysis from KTO's raw data (2006)

Travellers to Hong Kong who reported their purpose of visit as pleasure also mentioned that price was a motivating factor because there was no difference in travel cost, compared to domestic travel. The following table details the main reason of travel to Hong Kong by pleasure travellers.

The Main Reason of Travel (%)

	1st Choice	2nd Choice
There is no difference in travel cost, compared to domestic travel	31.7	9.5
I have visited almost all destinations in Republic of Korea	18.5	4.5
A place that I want to visit	18.1	22.6
Sense of satisfaction with overseas travel	9.1	9.1
Having opportunities for group travel	4.5	31.7
Others	18.1	

Source: Analysis from KTO's raw data (2006)

Pleasure travellers to Hong Kong reported engaging in a number of activities including city sightseeing and shopping, followed by enjoyment of natural scenery, and nightlife/entertainment (12.6%). The 10 most frequently indicated activities are listed in the table below:

Activities for Pleasure Travellers to Hong Kong (%)

Natural Scenery	17.7
Historic Monuments	6.3
Cultural Events/Festivals	5.1
Nightlife/Entertainment	12.6
Swimming/Sunbathing	1.3
Hiking/Camping	2.5
City Sightseeing	26.2
Business	2.5
Shopping	24.1
Others	1.7

Source: Analysis from KTO's raw data (2006)

Travel type to Hong Kong

Independent travellers are the dominant mode of travel of the Korean outbound tourists to Hong Kong (68.9%) as indicated in the table below:

Travel Type (%)

Independent Travel	68.9
Package Travel	31.1
Total	**100.0**

Source: Analysis from KTO's raw data (2006)

Satisfaction rate

Korean visitors to Hong Kong generally reported satisfaction with their overall visit. A very small number of respondents reported being dissatisfied. The main reason for being dissatisfied is related to "expensive travel product."

Korean visitors to Hong Kong reported various degrees of satisfaction and dissatisfaction depending upon the tourism sector. The degree of satisfaction or dissatisfaction by sector is detailed in the tables below: accommodation, food, shopping items, tour guide service, and tour itinerary. Korean visitors to Hong Kong generally reported being satisfied with their experience in terms of all these sectors.

Satisfaction Level by Sector (%)

	Accommodation	Food	Shopping Items	Guide Service	Tour Itinerary and Content
Very satisfied	4.5	9.1	13.6	4.5	0.0
Somewhat satisfied	50.2	41.2	50.2	32.1	45.3
Neutral	31.7	40.7	18.1	4.5	45.7
Somewhat dissatisfied	4.5	9.0	0.0	0.0	4.5
Very dissatisfied	9.1	0.0	0.0	0.0	0.0
I don't know	0.0	0.0	18.1	58.9	4.5
Total	**100.0**	**100.0**	**100.0**	**100.0**	**100.0**

Source: Analysis from KTO's raw data (2006)

Travel inconveniences

Korean visitors to Hong Kong indicated the language barrier to be the major travel inconvenience encountered during their visit. Food and local transportation were the second major travel inconvenience indicated, but in comparison feature as a minor source of concern. All 7 kinds of travel inconvenience are listed in the table below:

Travel Inconveniences (%)

Language Barrier	27.8
Travel Information	4.0
Local Transportation	8.0

Forced Employee Tips	4.0
Nightlife/Entertainment	4.0
Food	8.0
Criminal/Safety	4.0
Nothing	40.2
Total	**100.0**

Source: Analysis from KTO's raw data (2006)

3.1.4 India

Existing traffic and traffic patterns

India is the least frequently visited destination in the Asian region for Korean outbound travellers included in this report. 35,508 people visited India in 2005. A large majority of Korean travellers to India is male. The following table indicates the total numbers, percentage change and percentage share of Korean departures by gender to India from 2001 to 2005.

Korean Departures by Gender to India, 2001-2005

Year	Total		Male			Female		
	Number	+/- (%)	Number	+/- (%)	Share (%)	Number	+/- (%)	Share (%)
2001	18,091	18.0	11,872	15.6	65.6	6,219	22.7	34.4
2002	19,507	7.8	12,905	8.7	66.1	6,602	6.2	33.9
2003	26,071	33.6	17,439	35.1	66.9	8,632	30.8	33.1
2004	31,471	20.7	20,700	18.7	65.8	10,771	24.8	34.2
2005	35,508	12.8	23,168	11.9	65.3	12,340	14.6	34.7

Source: Analysis from KTO's raw data (2006)

Koreans visited India for business and pleasure. In 2005, 8.7% of travellers to India indicated pleasure as the main purpose of their visit.

Growth of Korean Departures by Purpose to India, 2001-2005

Category	2001		2002		2003		2004		2005	
	Number	+/- (%)	Number	+/- (%)	Number	+/- (%)	Number	+/- (%)	Number	+/- (%)
Pleasure	7,845	26.7	8,207	4.6	11,949	45.6	15,441	29.2	16,783	8.7
Business	6,853	9.4	7,040	2.7	8,951	27.1	10,943	22.3	13,173	20.4
VFR*	1,145	-2.4	1,108	-3.2	1,240	11.9	1,553	25.2	2,069	33.2
Official	108	-29.9	113	4.6	149	31.9	256	71.8	199	-22.3
Convention	312	59.2	417	33.7	280	-32.9	431	53.9	527	22.3
Others	1,828	26.1	2,622	43.4	3,502	33.6	2,847	-18.7	2,757	-3.2

* Excluding crew members
Source: Analysis from KTO's raw data (2006)

Most visitors to India are self-employed people from the private sector. The following table illustrates the details of Korean departures by occupation to India from 2001 to 2005.

Growth of Korean Departures by Occupation to India, 2001-2005

Category	2001		2002		2003		2004		2005	
	Number	+/- (%)	Number	+/- (%)	Number	+/- (%)	Number	+/- (%)	Number	+/- (%)
Official	215	48.3	242	12.6	300	24.0	494	64.7	485	-1.8
Private Sector	–	–	8,624	–	12,976	50.5	14,677	13.1	16,727	14
Self-Employed	542	37.9	590	8.9	665	12.7	750	12.8	1,016	35.5
Educator	–	–	817	–	1,206	47.6	1,480	22.7	1,788	20.8
Student	–	–	4,067	–	4,608	13.3	5,956	29.3	6,817	14.5
Others	–	–	1,405	–	1,457	3.7	1,720	18.1	1,893	10.1
Unemployed	–	–	3,896	–	4,990	28.1	6,552	31.3	6,952	6.1

Source: Analysis from KTO's raw data (2006)

Most travellers to India are in their thirties (9,810 for the year 2005), followed closely by those in their twenties and in their forties. The detailed breakdown of Korean departures by age to India is contained in the table below for the years 2001 to 2005.

Growth of Korean Departures by Age to India, 2001-2005

Category	2001		2002		2003		2004		2005	
	Number	+/- (%)	Number	+/- (%)	Number	+/- (%)	Number	+/- (%)	Number	+/- (%)
0 – 20	1,603	11.6	1,911	19.2	2,372	24.1	2,937	23.8	3,686	25.5
21 – 30	4,628	36.4	5,126	10.8	5,996	17.0	7,727	28.9	8,549	10.6
31 – 40	5,611	18.4	5,448	-2.9	7,811	43.4	8,790	12.5	9,810	11.6
41 – 50	4,062	10.5	4,579	12.7	6,460	41.1	7,488	15.9	8,432	12.6
51 – 60	1,575	4.0	1,713	8.8	2,429	41.8	3,231	33.0	3,678	13.8
>61	707	4.1	864	22.2	1,134	31.3	1,456	28.4	1,523	4.6

Source: Analysis from KTO's raw data (2006)

The following information has been analyzed from interviews with tour operators, travel agencies and airlines, as well as related websites:

Evaluation of Existing Traffic and Traffic Patterns in India

Category	Contents
Ease of entry	• Visa requirement for entering India
Accommodation	• Various kinds of accommodation • Retiring room, Dharamshala for pilgrims, guest house, lodge, luxury hotels etc.
Local transportation	• Various types of trains • Domestic flights • Motorcycle, bicycle and rickshaw are popular

Category	Contents		
Health, medical and insurance facilities	• Mineral water advisable for drinking • Growing medical industry		
Security	• Not seen as safe		
Food	• Most of the Indian cuisine is vegetarian • Curry is popular • Use the right hand when eating		
Telecommunications	• Easy to use telecommunication facilities • Telecommunication industry is developed		
Recreation and entertainment	• Movie theater • Yoga and meditation		
Tourism products	• Backpacking, pilgrimage, yoga tours, • India-Nepal connection tour		
Flight Schedule	**Route**	**Korean Airline**	**Asiana Airline**
	Incheon – Mumbai	3 flights/week	–
	Incheon – Dehli	–	3 flights/week

Source: Korean Airline, Asiana Airline, Tourism of India, Embassy of India in the Republic of Korea

Factors affecting destination selection

For Koreans, major information sources affecting the decision to travel to India include the recommendations of friends or relatives, business purposes, or package travel advertisement. More than 30% of Korean travellers to India reported the recommendations of friend or relatives as the major factor affecting their travel decision. Korean travellers want to visit India which is not well known to Korean people. However, more Koreans are becoming interested in visiting India which is seen as a mysterious destination. The major information source for travel to India is the internet. All major factors affecting the travel decision, and travel information sources are listed below:

Factors Affecting Destination Selection (%)

Package Travel advertisement by Travel Agency	6.7
Friends/Relatives Recommendation	33.2
Internet	6.7
Favorable Destination Image	6.7
Price	6.7
Business Related	40.0
Total	**100.0**

Source: Analysis from KTO's raw data (2006)

Travel Information Sources (%)

Travel Agencies	13.3
People with Overseas Travel Experiences	26.7
Guidebooks	13.3
Internet	46.7
Total	**100.0**

Source: Analysis from KTO's raw data (2006)

The purpose of travel

Outbound tourists to India reported their purpose of visit as leisure or relaxation and as well as business. In the table below, respondents' first and second responses indicate that leisure and/or relaxation is a second purpose for most Korean visitors to India.

The Purpose of Travel, First Choice Response (%)

	1st Choice	2nd Choice
Leisure/Relaxation	46.7	53.3
Business	46.6	6.7
Convention	6.7	6.7
Cultural/Sports	–	–
Others	–	–

Source: Analysis from KTO's raw data (2006)

Travellers to India who reported their purpose of visit as pleasure also reported their main purpose for visiting India as "a place that they had specifically wanted to visit". 60% made this their first response and almost 27% of these visitors indicated their sense of satisfaction with overseas travel as a second response. The table below details the types of responses indicated by pleasure travellers to India. Pleasure travellers to India reported engaging in a number of activities including the enjoyment of natural scenery and historic monuments. The eight most frequently indicated activities are listed thereafter. Choices of travel type by outbound tourists to India are independent travel type (73.3%), compared to 26.7% of package travel. The specific type of travel to India for Koreans is for business or backpacking.

The Main Reason of Travel (%)

	1st Choice	2nd Choice
There is no difference in travel cost, compared to domestic travel	6.7	6.7
A place that I specifically wanted to visit	60.0	26.7
Not many tourist attractions inRepublic of Korea	6.7	13.3
Sense of satisfaction with overseas travel	26.7	26.7

Source: Analysis from KTO's raw data (2006)

Activities for Pleasure Travellers to India (%)

Natural Scenery	22.4
Historic Monuments	17.9
Cultural Events/Festivals	7.5
Nightlife/Entertainment	7.5
Swimming/Sunbathing	1.5
Hiking/Camping	6.0
City Sightseeing	19.4
Shopping	17.8
Total	**100.0**

Source: Analysis from KTO's raw data (2006)

Satisfaction rate

Korean visitors to India reported various degrees of satisfaction and dissatisfaction depending upon the tourism sector. The degree of satisfaction or dissatisfaction by sector is detailed in the table below: accommodation, food, shopping items, tour guide service, and tour itinerary. Korean visitors to India generally reported being satisfied with their experience in terms of all these sectors.

Satisfaction Level by Sector (%)

	Accommodation	Food	Shopping Items	Guide Service	Tour Itinerary and Contents
Very satisfied	6.7	0.0	6.0	0.0	6.7
Somewhat satisfied	33.3	13.4	20.0	33.3	60.0
Neutral	46.6	26.6	30.3	33.3	20.0
Somewhat dissatisfied	6.7	53.3	13.4	0.0	6.6
Very dissatisfied	6.7	6.7	13.3	0.0	6.7
I don't know	0.0	0.0	17.0	33.4	0.0

Travel inconveniences

Korean visitors to India indicated the language barrier and food as the major travel inconveniences encountered during their visit. All eight kinds of travel inconvenience are listed below:

Travel Inconveniences (%)

Language Barrier	28.6
Money Exchange	3.6
Airline Reservation	3.6
Travel Information	14.3
Local Transportation	7.1

Food	25.0
Criminal/Safety	7.1
Severe pollution	3.6
Nothing	7.1
Total	**100.0**

Source: Analysis from KTO's raw data (2006)

3.1.5 Indonesia

Existing traffic and traffic patterns

Indonesia is a growing destination in the Asian region for Korean outbound travel. The table below indicates the total numbers, percentage change and percentage share of Korean departures by gender to Indonesia from 2001 to 2005. Male Korean travellers have a bigger market segment than female Korean travellers.

Korean Departures by Gender to Indonesia, 2001-2005

Year	Total		Male			Female		
	Number	+/- (%)	Number	+/- (%)	Share (%)	Number	+/- (%)	Share (%)
2001	92,580	49.4	59,010	35.3	63.7	33,570	82.9	36.3
2002	110,848	19.7	70,352	19.2	63.5	40,496	20.6	36.5
2003	105,267	-5.0	66,852	-5.0	63.5	38,415	-5.1	36.5
2004	124,828	18.6	73,890	10.5	59.2	50,938	32.6	40.8
2005	125,980	0.9	75,540	2.2	59.6	50,440	-1.0	40.4

Source: Analysis from KTO's raw data (2006

Koreans have consistently visited Indonesia for pleasure since 2001. As indicated in the table below, 80,357 travellers to Indonesia indicated pleasure as the main purpose of their visit, a 1% decrease due to the Bali bombing incidents in 2005.

Growth of Korean Departures by Purpose to Indonesia, 2001-2005

Category	2001		2002		2003		2004		2005	
	Number	+/- (%)	Number	+/- (%)	Number	+/- (%)	Number	+/- (%)	Number	+/- (%)
Pleasure	47,567	117.3	60,332	26.8	60,364	0.1	81,198	34.5	80,357	-1.0
Business	28,829	13.7	30,568	6.0	27,258	-10.8	27,203	-0.2	26,967	-0.9
VFR*	8,828	7.7	10,605	20.1	10,559	-0.4	10,335	-2.1	11,855	14.7
Official	1,071	-24.3	760	-29	580	-23.7	319	-45.0	497	55.8
Convention	846	78.1	933	10.3	714	-23.5	526	-26.3	682	29.7
Others	5,439	17.6	7,650	40.7	5,792	-24.3	5,247	-9.4	4,622	-11.9

Source: Analysis from KTO's raw data (2006)

Most visitors to Indonesia are official and private sector's employees. Except these segments, travellers by occupation have decreased due to safety and security issues. The following table illustrates the details of Korean departures by occupation to Indonesia from 2001 to 2005:

Growth of Korean Departures by Occupation to Indonesia, 2001-2005

Category	2001		2002		2003		2004		2005	
	Number	+/- (%)	Number	+/- (%)	Number	+/- (%)	Number	+/- (%)	Number	+/- (%)
Official	1,521	-10.1	1,320	-13.2	1,318	-0.2	1,209	-8.3	1,343	11.1
Private Sector	–	–	51,488	–	48,693	-5.4	54,848	12.6	52,841	3.7
Self-Employed	5,564	74.2	6,053	8.8	6,000	-0.9	6,085	1.4	5,838	-4.1
Educator	–	–	1,933	–	2,080	7.6	2,311	11.1	2,187	-5.4
Student	–	–	9,107	–	8,912	-2.1	10,307	15.7	9,687	-6.0
Others	–	–	5,780	–	4,564	-21	5,093	11.6	5,184	1.8
Unemployed	–	–	36,003	–	34,342	-4.6	45,653	32.9	48,579	6.4

Source: Analysis from KTO's raw data (2006)

Most travellers to Indonesia are in their thirties (35,787 for the year 2005), followed by those in their forties. The detailed breakdown of Korean departures by age to Indonesia is contained in the table below, for the years 2001 to 2005:

Growth of Korean Departures by Age to Indonesia, 2001-2005

Category	2001		2002		2003		2004		2005	
	Number	+/- (%)	Number	+/- (%)	Number	+/- (%)	Number	+/- (%)	Number	+/- (%)
0 – 20	10,312	68.4	11,300	9.6	10,947	-3.1	13,651	24.7	14,122	3.5
21 – 30	18,354	59.6	21,892	19.3	20,958	-4.3	27,168	29.6	27,265	0.4
31 – 40	26,509	38.9	31,237	17.8	29,917	-4.2	33,837	13.0	35,787	5.8
41 – 50	23,822	45.6	29,788	25.0	27,657	-7.2	30,368	9.8	29,592	-2.6
51 – 60	10,252	49.9	12,178	18.8	12,242	0.5	14,471	18.2	13,255	-8.4
> 61	4,104	65.6	5,289	28.9	5,188	-1.9	6,011	15.9	5,638	-6.2

Source: KTO

The following data has been obtained from interviews with tour operators, travel agencies and airlines, Tourism Indonesia, and Indonesian Embassy in the Republic of Korea as well as related websites:

Evaluation of Existing Traffic and Traffic Patterns

Category	Contents
Ease of entry	• Visa on Arrival
Accommodation	• Various levels of hotels • Many luxury hotels and resorts are in Bali
Local transportation	• Bajai and Ojek are popular • Bus and taxi can be used

Health, medical and insurance facilities	• Not up to expected standard of medical service in the Republic of Korea		
Security	• Not quite safe		
Food	• Rice is the main staple • Extensive use of spices		
Telecommunications	• Growing telecommunication industry • Telephone, fax, internet can be used in major hotels or offices		
Tour products	• Honeymoon for Bali and Bintan • Golf tours, city tours for Jakarta		
Flight Schedule	**Route**	**Korean Airline**	**Asiana Airline**
	Incheon – Jakarta	7 flights/week	–

Source: Korean Airline, Asiana Airline, Tourism of Indonesia

Factors affecting destination selection

For Koreans, major information sources affecting the decision to travel to Indonesia include package travel advertisement or the recommendations of friends or relatives. The main information source for travel to Indonesia (over 34%) was from travel agencies. All major factors affecting the travel decision and a list of travel information source are listed below:

Factors Affecting Destination Selection (%)

Package Travel Advertisement	34.9
NTO Promotion	6.4
Friends/Relatives Recommendation	33.2
Business	25.5
Total	**100.0**

Source: Analysis from KTO's raw data (2006)

Travel Information Sources (%)

Travel Agency	34.3
People with Overseas Travel Experiences	26.1
Mass Media	12.8
Internet	26.8
Total	**100.0**

Source: Analysis from KTO's raw data (2006)

The purpose of travel

Outbound tourists to Indonesia reported their purpose of visit as honeymoon (41.9%) and leisure or relaxation (26.1%). In the following table, respondents' first and second responses indicate that leisure or relaxation is a second purpose for most Korean visitors to Indonesia.

The Purpose of Travel (%)

	1st Choice	2nd Choice
Leisure/Relaxation	26.1	73.9
VFR	6.4	–
Business	19.2	–
Training	6.4	–
Honeymoon	41.9	–
Total	**100.0**	**–**

Source: Analysis from KTO's raw data (2006)

Travellers to Indonesia who reported their purpose of visit as pleasure also reported their main purpose for visiting Indonesia as "there is no difference in travel cost, compared to domestic travel". The table below details the types of responses indicated by pleasure travellers to Indonesia. Pleasure travellers to Indonesia reported engaging in a number of activities including the enjoyment of natural scenery and city sightseeing. The 10 most frequently indicated activities are listed in the table thereafter. Choices of travel type by outbound tourists to Indonesia are package travel type (61.1%) followed by independent travel (38.9%).

The Main Reason of Travel (%)

	1st Choice	2nd Choice
There is no difference in travel cost, compared to domestic travel	48.9	24.4
A place that I want to visit	26.7	51.2
Having opportunities for group travel	24.4	24.4
Total	**100.0**	**100.0**

Source: Analysis from KTO's raw data (2006)

Activities for Pleasure Travellers to Indonesia (%)

Natural Scenery	18.3
Historic Monuments	7.3
Cultural Events/Festivals	5.5
Nightlife/Entertainment	17.0
Swimming/Sunbathing	12.7
Hiking/Camping	1.5
Golf	2.7
City Sightseeing	16.6
Business	1.4
Shopping	17.0
Total	**100.0**

Source: Analysis from KTO's raw data (2006)

Satisfaction rate

Korean visitors to Indonesia were generally satisfied with their overall visit. A very small number of respondents reported being dissatisfied. The main reasons for being dissatisfied are due to unclean accommodations and surroundings.

Korean visitors to Indonesia reported various degrees of satisfaction and dissatisfaction depending upon the tourism sector. The degree of satisfaction or dissatisfaction by sector is detailed in the table below: accommodation, food, shopping items, tour guide service, tour itinerary and contents. Korean visitors to Indonesia generally reported being satisfied with their experience in terms of all these sectors.

Satisfaction Level by Sector (%)

	Accommodation	Food	Shopping Items	Guide Service	Tour Itinerary and Contents
Very satisfied	14.0	0.0	7.0	21.0	21.0
Somewhat satisfied	47.7	34.3	27.3	33.7	19.8
Neutral	25.5	46.5	52.9	13.4	52.9
Somewhat dissatisfied	6.4	19.2	0.0	0.0	6.3
Very dissatisfied	0.0	0.0	0.0	0.0	0.0
I don't know	6.4	0.0	12.8	31.9	0.0
Total	**100.0**	**100.0**	**100.0**	**100.0**	**100.0**

Travel inconveniences

Korean visitors to Indonesia indicated cash exchange as the major travel inconvenience encountered during their visit, while the language barrier was the first major travel inconvenience indicated. Meanwhile, almost 25% of respondents indicated that they have not encountered any travel inconvenience during their stay in Indonesia. All eight kinds of travel inconvenience are listed below:

Travel Inconveniences (%)

Language Barrier	29.9
Cash Exchange	5.2
Travel Information	5.2
Local Transportation	9.5
Forced Employee Tips	5.2
Food	10.0
Guide Tips	5.2
Airplane Transfer	5.2
Nothing	24.6
Total	**100.0**

Source: Analysis from KTO's raw data (2006)

3.1.6 Japan

Existing traffic and traffic patterns

Japan is a favorite destination in the Asian region for Korean outbound travellers. As mentioned earlier in the report, 1,739,424 people or 19.1% of the Republic of Korea's outbound market visited Japan in 2005. However, even though more female Koreans are traveling abroad, there are more Korean males visiting Japan. The following table indicates the total number, percentage change and percentage share of Korean departures by gender to Japan from 2001 to 2005.

Korean Departures by Gender to Japan, 2001-2005

Year	Total		Male			Female		
	Number	+/- (%)	Number	+/- (%)	Share (%)	Number	+/- (%)	Share (%)
2001	1,169,620	6.2	636,041	4.4	54.4	533,579	8.5	45.6
2002	1,266,116	8.3	684,024	7.5	54	582,092	9.1	46.0
2003	1,427,331	12.7	766,504	12.1	53.7	660,827	13.5	46.3
2004	1,569,175	9.9	836,876	9.2	53.3	732,299	10.8	46.7
2005	1,739,424	10.8	923,967	10.4	53.1	815,457	11.4	46.9

Source: Analysis from KTO's raw data (2006)

Koreans have consistently visited Japan for pleasure rather than business since 2001. As indicated in the following table, 15.4% of travellers to Japan indicated pleasure as the main purpose of their visit in 2005. The reported purpose for visiting is for pleasure, followed by business and visiting friends and relatives

Growth of Korean Departures by Purpose to Japan, 2001-2005

Category	2001		2002		2003		2004		2005	
	Number	+/- (%)	Number	+/- (%)	Number	+/- (%)	Number	+/- (%)	Number	+/- (%)
Pleasure	467,413	16.1	588,947	26	757,557	30.2	882,789	16.5	1,018,562	15.4
Business	350,365	3.7	328,527	-6.2	334,025	1.7	346,045	3.6	361,089	4.4
VFR*	219,089	-5.3	202,223	-7.7	198,515	-1.8	192,197	-3.2	211,985	10.3
Official	3,954	0.2	6,277	58.8	4,293	-31.6	4,348	1.3	4,312	-0.8
Convention	15,917	6.2	17,337	8.9	15,490	-10.7	22,661	46.3	18,302	-19.2
Others	112,882	2.1	122,805	8.8	117,451	-4.4	121,135	3.1	125,174	3.3

* Excluding crew members
Source: Analysis from KTO's raw data (2006)

Most visitors to Japan are people employed in the private sector, although this number is followed closely by those who are unemployed, mostly housewives who make up an important growing demographic segment of the Republic of Korea's outbound tourist market. The following table illustrates the details of Korean departures by occupation to Japan from 2001 to 2005.

Growth of Korean Departures by Occupation to Japan, 2001-2005

Category	2001		2002		2003		2004		2005	
	Number	+/- (%)	Number	+/- (%)	Number	+/- (%)	Number	+/- (%)	Number	+/- (%)
Official	12,285	10.3	17,030	38.6	19,377	13.8	21,556	11.5	21,536	-0.1
Private Sector	–	–	489,829	–	555,627	13.4	611,728	10.1	678,600	10.9
Self-Employed	92,906	0.1	96,237	3.6	99,707	3.6	100,435	0.7	105,827	5.4
Educator	–	–	40,642	–	50,757	24.9	57,453	13.2	61,171	6.5
Student	–	–	187,778	–	232,705	23.9	267,177	14.8	299,493	12.1
Others	–	–	233,576	–	221,918	-5.0	238,375	7.4	230,804	-3.2
Unemployed	–	–	375,900	–	408,816	8.8	443,095	8.4	502,860	13.5

Source: Analysis from KTO's raw data (2006)

Most travellers to Japan are in their thirties (443,660 for the year 2005), followed closely by those in their twenties and in their forties. The detailed breakdown of Korean departures by age to Japan is contained in the following table for the years 2001 to 2005.

Growth of Korean Departures by Age to Japan, 2001-2005

Category	2001		2002		2003		2004		2005	
	Number	+/- (%)	Number	+/- (%)	Number	+/- (%)	Number	+/- (%)	Number	+/- (%)
0 – 20	119,922	10.4	144,450	20.5	177,255	22.7	201,742	13.8	216,791	7.5
21 – 30	258,152	7.9	265,520	2.9	298,844	12.6	335,669	12.3	395,825	17.9
31 – 40	341,951	3.5	351,048	2.7	374,310	6.6	404,288	8.0	443,660	9.7
41 – 50	277,183	7.4	304,342	9.8	335,281	10.2	361,466	7.8	391,024	8.2
51 – 60	175,298	4.1	188,861	7.7	209,551	11.0	226,553	8.1	246,202	8.7
>61	166,248	1.9	186,771	12.3	193,666	3.7	210,101	8.5	206,789	-1.6

Source: Analysis from KTO's raw data (2006)

The following information was obtained from interviews with tour operators, travel agencies and airlines, and Korean representative of Japan National Tourism Administration as well as related websites.

Evaluation of Japan's Existing Traffic and Traffic Pattern

Category	Contents
Ease of entry	• Visa is not required for Korean citizens
Accommodation	• Wide variety of accommodation at all levels • Ryokans, minsooks, pensions, youths hostels
Local transportation	• Sufficient domestic flights for transfers • Japan Rail Pass (JR), subways, taxis, buses
Health, medical and insurance facilities	• High quality medical center • Excellent welfare system
Security	• Most of the cities are safe and clean

Category	Contents		
Food	• Good variety of food • Sushi, sashimi, soba, sukiyaki etc.		
Telecommunications	• International call, fax, post, accessing internet are available and efficient		
Recreation and entertainment	• Spa tourism is popular • Many shopping center • Karaoke, digital games		
Tour products	• Honeymoon, school excursion, ski tour, spa, • Theme park, convention, incentive tour		
Flight Schedule	**Route**	**Korean Airline**	**Asiana Airline**
	Incheon – Kagoshima	3 flights/week	–
	Incheon – Komatsu	4 flights/week	–
	Incheon – Nagasaki	2 flights/week	–
	Incheon – Nagoya	21 flights/week	21 flights/week
	Busan – Nagoya	14 flights/week	–
	Jeju – Nagoya	5 flights/week	–
	Incheon – Niigata	7 flights/week	–
	Incheon – Tokyo(Narita)	49 flights/week	42 flights/week
	Busan – Tokyo(Narita)	7 flights/week	–
	Jeju – okyo(Narita)	7 flights/week	–
	Incheon – Tokyo(Haneda)	–	2 flights/week
	Incheon – Sapporo(Chitose)	7 flights/week	–
	Incheon – Aomori	4 flights/week	–
	Incheon – Akita	3 flights/week	–
	Incheon – Osaka(Kansai)	35 flights/week	28 flights/week
	Busan – Osaka(Kansai)	7 flights/week	7 flights/week
	Jeju – Osaka(Kansai)	7 flights/week	–
	Incheon – Oita	2 flights/week	–
	Incheon – Okayam	7 flights/week	–
	Incheon – Fukuoka	19 flights/week	13 flights/week
	Busan – Fukuoka	7 flights/week	2 flights/week
	Jeju – Fukuoka	2 flights/week	3 flights/week
	Incheon – Kumamoto	–	3 flights/week
	Incheon – Takamatsu	–	3 flights/week
	Incheon – Toyama	–	5 flights/week
	Incheon – Matsuyama	–	3 flights/week
	Incheon – Miyazaki	–	3 flights/week

Category	Contents		
Flight Schedule	Incheon – Sendai	–	7 flights/week
	Incheon – Okinawa	–	5 flights/week
	Incheon – Yonago	–	3 flights/week
	Incheon – Fukushima	–	5 flights/week
	Incheon – Hiroshima	–	7 flights/week

Factors affecting destination selection

For Koreans, major information sources affecting the decision to travel to Japan include the recommendations of friends or relatives, business reasons, or package travel advertisement. More than 30% of Korean travellers to Japan reported the recommendations of friends or relatives as the major factor affecting their travel decision. Koreans' decision to visit Japan is largely affected by the recommendations of friends and relatives, or by business considerations. They rely on the experiences of friends and relatives to inform them regarding their travel choices, but the internet is quickly becoming a major information source. Travel agencies converting their operations to e-business can capitalize on this trend by offering information and travel products to the same source. All major factors affecting the travel decision are listed below:

Factors Affecting Destination Selection (%)

Package Travel Ads	15.9
NTO Promotion	2.9
Friends/Relatives Recommendation	30.7
Internet	6.5
Destination Image	13.4
Mass Media	1.6
Prices	2.2
Business	26.8
Total	**100.0**

Source: Analysis from KTO's report and Results from Stakeholders' Interviews

The purpose of travel

Outbound tourists going to Japan reported their purpose of visit as leisure and/or relaxation. Honeymoon, school excursions and other incentive tour programs attract Korean travellers from every age bracket, indicating that Japan is a mature and well-developed destination for the Korean outbound market.

The Purpose of Travel (%)

Purpose of Travel	1st Choice	2nd Choice
Leisure/Relaxation	47.2	49.8
VFR	10.0	3.9
Business	24.6	0.5

Purpose of Travel	1st Choice	2nd Choice
Convention	3.8	0.5
Training	10.9	0.8
Culture/Sports Activities	2.6	1.1
Honeymoon	0.6	0.2
Others	0.3	43.2

Source: Analysis from KTO's report and Results from Stakeholders' Interviews

Travellers to Japan who reported their purpose of visit as pleasure also reported their main purpose for visiting Japan as a place that they had specifically wanted to visit. Almost 44% made this their first response. The following table details the reasons to travel indicated by pleasure travellers to Japan:

Main Reason to Travel (%)

	1st Choice	2nd Choice
There is no difference in travel cost, compared to domestic travel	16.2	11.9
A place that I want to visit	43.4	24.8
Not many tourist attractions in Republic of Korea	3.3	4.9
Sense of satisfaction with overseas travel	18.7	27.5
Not many entertainment facilities in Korea	1.1	2.0
Having opportunities for Group Travel	6.0	3.2
Others	7.0	0.2
Others	4.3	8.0

Source: Analysis from KTO's report and Results from Stakeholders' Interviews

Pleasure travellers to Japan reported engaging in a number of activities including city sightseeing (21.6%), shopping (20.8%), followed by enjoyment of natural scenery (20.7%) and historic monuments (15.1%), nightlife/entertainment (11.3%), and cultural events/festivals (5.%). The 14 indicated activities are listed below:

Activities for Pleasure Travellers to Japan (%)

Natural Scenery	20.7
Historic Monuments	15.1
Cultural Events/Festivals	5.0
Hot Springs	1.0
Nightlife/Entertainment	11.3
Swimming/Sunbathing	0.3
Hiking/Camping	1.0
Golf	0.4
Ski	0.0
Casino	0.1
City Sightseeing	21.6

Business Trip	2.6
Shopping	20.9
Others	0.0
Total	**100.0**

Source: Analysis from KTO's report and Results from Stakeholders' Interviews

Package vs. FIT

Choices of travel type by outbound tourists to Japan are almost evenly distributed between independent travel type and package travel type. There are slightly more independent travels (53.8%) than package travels (46.2%). It can be explained by the number of Korean-Japanese people living in Japan. The specific type of travel to Japan for Koreans is for visiting friends and relatives (25.5%), for business (24.3%), or for package travel (24.9%). Even though Korean FITs to Japan have increased, traditionally Korean travellers, in particular, the over 40s' prefer package travel. Interestingly, SMERF (Social, Military, Education, Religion and Fraternity) group is becoming a significant segment among Korean outbound travellers visiting Japanese destinations. The range of specific types of travel to Japan is detailed in the following table:

Specific Type of Travel (%)

VFR	25.5
Business	24.3
Backpacking	2.6
Official	1.4
Package	24.9
SMERF Group	10.1
SMERF Independence	5.2
Training	6.0
Total	100.0

Source: Analysis from KTO's report and Results from Stakeholders' Interviews

Satisfaction rate

Korean visitors to Japan generally reported satisfaction with their overall visit, with only a very small number of respondents reported being dissatisfied. The main reasons for being dissatisfied are related to the high expense of food and accommodation.

Korean visitors to Japan reported various degrees of satisfaction and dissatisfaction depending upon the tourism sector. The degree of satisfaction or dissatisfaction by sector is detailed in the table below: accommodation, food, shopping items, tour guide's service, and tour itinerary. Korean visitors to Japan generally reported being satisfied with their experience in terms of all these sectors.

Satisfaction Level by Sector (%)

	Accommodation	Food	Shopping Items	Guide Service	Tour Itinerary
Very satisfied	7.7	4.7	6.2	5.4	7.8
Somewhat satisfied	58.2	52.0	54.2	30.7	50.7

	Accommodation	Food	Shopping Items	Guide Service	Tour Itinerary
Neutral	18.5	29.6	27.0	17.3	33.5
Somewhat dissatisfied	4.0	10.9	3.0	2.1	2.4
Very dissatisfied	0.5	2.3	0.8	0.3	0.3
I don't know	11.1	0.5	8.8	44.2	5.3
Total	100.0	100.0	100.0	100.0	100.0

Source: Analysis from KTO's report and Results from Stakeholders' Interviews

Travel inconveniences

Korean visitors to Japan almost unanimously indicated the language barrier (38.2%) as the major travel inconvenience encountered during their visit. Food (11.6%) was the second major travel inconvenience indicated. Almost 33% of respondents indicated that they encountered no travel inconvenience. All 18 kinds of travel inconvenience are listed below:

Travel Inconveniences (%)

Category	
Language Barrier	38.4
Money Exchange	1.0
Airplane Reservation	1.0
Tour Information	2.2
Information Desk Service	0.3
Local Transportation	7.2
Forced Employee Tips	0.3
Forced Sale	0.7
Nightlife/Entertainment	1.4
Food	11.6
Criminal/Safety	0.9
Forced the additional Expenditure of Travel Agency	0.7
Guide Tips	1.1
Airplane Transfer	0.1
Not using Credit Card	0.1
Expenditure Price	0.3
Rip-off	0.1
Nothing	32.6
Total	100.0

Source: Analysis from KTO's report and Results from Stakeholders' Interviews

3.1.7 Malaysia

Existing traffic and traffic patterns

Malaysia is one of the most preferred destinations in the Asian region for Korean outbound travellers. As mentioned earlier in the report, 97,694 people or 17.4% of the Republic of Korea's outbound market visited Malaysia in 2005. The following table indicates the total numbers, percentage change and percentage share of Korean departures by gender to Malaysia from 2001 to 2005.

Korean Departures by Gender to Malaysia, 2001-2005

Year	Total		Male			Female		
	Number	+/- (%)	Number	+/- (%)	Share (%)	Number	+/- (%)	Share (%)
2001	51,469	1.1	32,483	-0.6	63.1	18,986	4.0	36.9
2002	55,654	8.1	35,163	8.3	63.2	20,491	7.9	36.8
2003	59,929	7.7	37,798	7.5	63.1	22,131	8.0	36.9
2004	83,200	38.8	51,292	35.7	61.7	31,908	44.2	38.3
2005	97,694	17.4	57,955	13.0	59.3	39,739	24.5	40.7

Source: Analysis from KTO's raw data (2006)

Koreans have consistently visited Malaysia for pleasure rather than business since 2001. As indicated in the following table, 18.4% of travellers to Malaysia indicated pleasure as the main purpose of their visit in 2005.

Growth of Korean Departures by Purpose to Malaysia, 2001-2005

Category	2001		2002		2003		2004		2005	
	Number	+/- (%)	Number	+/- (%)	Number	+/- (%)	Number	+/- (%)	Number	+/- (%)
Pleasure	25,791	-0.4	30,647	18.8	30,990	1.1	51,155	65.1	60,570	18.4
Business	17,032	-2.3	16,457	-3.4	17,608	7.0	20,018	13.7	20,526	2.5
VFR*	3,600	-8.2	3,711	3.1	4,564	23.0	5,809	27.3	7,767	33.7
Official	226	61.4	237	4.9	308	30.0	276	-10.4	376	36.2
Convention	936	21.2	815	-12.9	2,426	197.7	1,140	-53.0	3,519	208.7
Others	3,884	40.5	3,787	-2.5	4,033	6.5	4,802	19.1	4,936	2.8

* Excluding crew members
Source: Analysis from KTO's raw data (2006)

Most visitors to Malaysia are people employed in the private sector, although this number is followed closely by those who are unemployed (housewives and retirees), mostly housewives who make up a quickly growing demographic segment of the Republic of Korea's outbound tourist market. The table below illustrates the details of Korean departures by occupation to Malaysia from 2001 to 2005.

Growth of Korean Departures by Occupation to Malaysia, 2001-2005

Category	2001		2002		2003		2004		2005	
	Number	+/- (%)	Number	+/- (%)	Number	+/- (%)	Number	+/- (%)	Number	+/- (%)
Official	632	41.1	700	10.8	767	9.6	865	12.8	1,052	21.6
Private sector	–	–	26,411	–	27,543	4.3	35,900	30.3	37,911	5.6
Self employed	2,617	6.0	2,757	5.4	3,528	28.0	4,100	16.2	4,628	12.9
Educator	–	–	1,206	–	1,285	6.6	2,010	56.4	2,086	3.8
Student	–	–	5,825	–	6,519	11.9	9,908	52.0	11,979	20.9
Others	–	–	3,276	–	3,036	-7.3	4,204	38.5	4,376	4.1
Unemployed	–	–	15,966	–	17,719	11.0	26,851	51.5	36,265	35.1

Source: Analysis from KTO's raw data (2006)

Most travellers to Malaysia are in their forties (32,184 for the year 2005), followed closely by those in their thirties. The detailed breakdown of Korean departures by age to Malaysia is shown in the table below, for the years 2001 to 2005.

Growth of Korean Departures by Age to Malaysia, 2001-2005

Category	2001		2002		2003		2004		2005	
	Number	+/- (%)	Number	+/- (%)	Number	+/- (%)	Number	+/- (%)	Number	+/- (%)
0 – 20	5,093	14.3	6,617	29.9	7,499	13.3	11,874	58.3	15,468	30.3
21 – 30	11,865	3.1	11,093	-6.5	10,058	-9.3	13,671	35.9	15,283	11.8
31 – 40	15,876	-0.1	16,679	5.1	18,744	12.4	24,736	32.0	28,619	15.7
41 – 50	25,098	5.9	27,378	9.1	30,192	10.3	30,448	0.8	32,184	5.7
51 – 60	5,182	-10.2	5,875	13.4	6,050	3.0	9,100	50.4	10,380	14.1
> 61	2,141	-12.0	2,652	23.9	2,740	3.3	4,746	73.2	6,217	31.0

Source: Analysis from KTO's raw data (2006)

The following information was obtained from interviews with tour operators, travel agencies and airlines, and Korean representative of Malaysia Tourism Promotion Board as well as related websites.

Evaluation of Existing Traffic and Traffic Patterns in Malaysia

Category	Contents
Ease of entry	• Visa on Arrival
Accommodation	• Various varieties of hotels and accommodation
Local transportation	• Kuala Lumpur has a good transportation system • Taxi, bus, LRT, KTM (train)
Health, medical and insurance facilities	• Medical industry is growing
Security	• Most of the tourist attractions are seen as safe
Food	• Large variety of international food and tropical fruits • Many open air restaurants

Category	Contents		
Telecommunications	• Easy to use telecommunication facilities • Development of the telecommunication industry		
Tour products	• Honeymoon destination for Kuala Lumpur, Penang • Golf tour, skin scuba in Kota Kinabalu • Climbing Mt. Kinabalu		
Flight Schedule	**Route**	**Korean Airline**	**Asiana Airline**
	Incheon – Penang	2 flights/week	–
	Incheon – Kuala Lumpur	13 flights/week	–
	Incheon – Kota Kinabalu	2 flights/week	4 flights/week

Source: Korean Airline, Asiana Airline Malaysia Tourism Promotion Board

Factors affecting destination selection

For Koreans, an important information source affecting the decision to travel to Malaysia is the internet. Outbound tourists going to Malaysia reported their purpose of travel as honeymoon.

Travellers to Malaysia who reported their purpose of visit also reported their main purpose for visiting Malaysia as "not many tourist attractions in the Republic of Korea." Travellers to Malaysia reported engaging in a number of activities including the enjoyment of natural scenery, historic monuments, city sightseeing, and shopping.

3.1.8 The Philippines

Existing traffic and traffic patterns

The Philippines is a destination that is only about half as popular as Thailand, with only a 5% share of the Korean outbound market. Koreans are six times more likely to visit China than the Philippines. 481,397 people visited the Philippines in 2005. There are more Korean males visiting the Philippines. The table below indicates the total number, percentage change and percentage share of Korean departures by gender to the Philippines from 2001 to 2005.

Korean Departures by Gender to the Philippines, 2001-2005

Year	Total		Male			Female		
	Number	**+/- (%)**	**Number**	**+/- (%)**	**Share (%)**	**Number**	**+/- (%)**	**Share (%)**
2001	203,682	25.8	118,596	21.5	58.2	85,086	32.3	41.8
2002	280,413	37.7	159,524	34.5	56.9	120,889	42.1	43.1
2003	293,099	4.5	168,477	5.6	57.5	124,622	3.1	42.5
2004	377,217	28.7	211,745	25.7	56.1	165,472	32.8	43.9
2005	481,397	27.6	267,939	26.5	55.7	213,458	29.0	44.3

Source: KTO Report 2005

Koreans have consistently visited the Philippines for pleasure rather than for business since 2001. As indicated in the following table, 29% of travellers to the Philippines in 2005, indicated pleasure as the main purpose of their visit.

Growth of Korean Departures by Purpose to the Philippines, 2001-2005

Category	2001		2002		2003		2004		2005	
	Number	+/- (%)	Number	+/- (%)	Number	+/- (%)	Number	+/- (%)	Number	+/- (%)
Pleasure	142,999	41.9	214,105	49.7	226,979	6.0	303,564	33.7	391,848	29.0
Business	30,748	-2.7	31,577	2.7	29,883	-5.4	31,150	4.2	32,103	3.0
VFR*	15,031	-4.6	17,462	16.2	20,659	18.3	24,247	17.4	34,644	42.9
Official	337	-18.4	1,001	297.0	973	-2.8	420	-56.8	629	49.8
Convention	1,344	-20.0	1,141	-15.1	1,010	-11.5	1,024	1.4	1,171	14.4
Others	13,223	12.9	15,127	14.4	13,595	-10.1	16,812	23.7	21,002	24.9

* Excluding crew members
Source: Analysis from KTO's raw data (2006)

Most visitors to the Philippines are unemployed or are people employed in the private sector. The table below illustrates the details of Korean departures by occupation to the Philippines from 2001 to 2005.

Growth of Korean Departures by Occupation to the Philippines, 2001-2005

Category	2001		2002		2003		2004		2005	
	Number	+/- (%)	Number	+/- (%)	Number	+/- (%)	Number	+/- (%)	Number	+/- (%)
Official	1,794	35.5	2,797	55.9	3,006	7.5	3,030	0.8	4,289	41.6
Private Sector	–	–	105,210	–	107,792	2.5	131,422	21.9	157,516	19.9
Self Employed	13,151	20.0	17,711	34.7	18,536	4.7	23,853	28.7	25,743	7.9
Educator	–	–	6,048	–	6,592	9.0	7,987	21.2	9,834	23.1
Student	–	–	32,640	–	35,601	9.1	50,659	42.3	68,072	34.4
Others	–	–	17,896	–	16,853	-5.8	19,996	18.7	20,673	3.4
Unemployed	–	–	99,523	–	106,140	6.7	141,668	33.5	196,831	38.9

Source: KTO (Korea Tourism Organization) Report 2005

Most travellers to the Philippines are in their twenties (137,057 for the year 2005), followed closely by those in their thirties or in their forties. The detailed breakdown of Korean departures by age to the Philippines can be seen in the following table for the years 2001 to 2005.

Growth of Korean Departures by Age to the Philippines, 2001-2005

Category	2001		2002		2003		2004		2005	
	Number	+/- (%)	Number	+/- (%)	Number	+/- (%)	Number	+/- (%)	Number	+/- (%)
0 – 20	23,143	-85.8	32,623	41.0	35,860	9.9	49,525	38.1	67,320	35.9
21 – 30	61,249	-62.4	81,910	33.7	80,115	-2.2	98,748	23.3	137,057	38.8
31 – 40	52,541	-67.8	72,572	38.1	75,731	4.4	94,337	24.6	119,851	27.1
41 – 50	40,580	-75.1	56,597	39.5	62,003	9.6	79,898	28.9	92,229	15.4
51 – 60	18,651	-88.6	25,765	38.1	27,996	8.7	37,997	35.7	44,309	16.6
> 61	8,596	-94.7	12,358	43.8	12,815	3.7	18,110	41.3	22,192	22.5

Source: KTO

The following information was obtained from interviews with tour operators, travel agencies and airlines, and Korean representative of The Philippine Tourism Organization as well as related websites.

Evaluation of Existing Traffic and Traffic Pattern in the Philippines

Category	Contents
Ease of entry	• No visa requirement if stay is less than 21 days
Accommodation	• Variety of accommodation • Many luxury hotels and resorts located on the islands
Local transportation	• Domestic flights for transfers • Inter-island service by ferry or boat • Jeep, bus, train, metro rail
Health, medical and insurance facilities	• Not up to expected standard of medical service in the Republic of Korea
Security	• Not seen as safe
Food	• Fresh seafood and fruits are abundant
Telecommunication	• International call, fax, post, accessing Internet are • Available and efficient
Recreation and entertainment	• Popular for clubs, and live band events • Night activities are common
Tour products	• Honeymoon for Manila, Cebu • Golf tour

Flight Schedule	Route	Korean Airline	Asiana Airline
	Incheon – Manila	13 flights/week	11 flights/week
	Incheon – Cebu	–	4 flights/week
	Incheon – Krake	–	5 flights/week

Source: Korean Airline, Asiana Airline, Embassy of Philippines in the Republic of Korea

Factors affecting destination selection

For Koreans, major information sources affecting the decision to travel to the Philippines include the recommendations of friends or relatives, business reasons, or package travel advertisement. More than 30% of Korean travellers to the Philippines reported the recommendations of friends or relatives as the major factor affecting their travel decision. This indicates that price and the availability of travel packages via travel agencies and the internet make the Philippines a small but potentially growing travel destination choice. People travel to the Philippines for business as well as for pleasure, and it is a destination that is not any more expensive than a similar domestic trip. All major factors affecting the travel decision are listed below:

Factors Affecting Destination Selection (%)

Package Travel Advertisement	27.7
NTO Promotion	0.8
Friends/Relatives Recommendation	31.2
Internet Search	13.4
Favorable Destination Image	9.3
Mass Media	0.8
Low Price	4.3
Business	12.5
Total	**100.0**

Source: Analysis from KTO's raw data (2006)

Travel information sources are listed below. Both travel agencies (31.8%) and the internet are the most preferred information sources to select the Philippines as a tourist destination, followed by recommendations from experienced travellers (31.3%), mass media, guidebooks, etc. It is related to young students and honeymooners, taking advantage of using travel agency and internet.

Travel Information Sources (%)

Travel Agency	31.8
People with Overseas Travel Experiences	31.3
Mass Media	1.7
Guidebooks	3.3
Internet	31.9
Total	**100.0**

Source: Analysis from KTO's raw data (2006)

The purpose of travel

Outbound tourists to the Philippines reported their purpose of visit as leisure or relaxation. The abundance of luxury hotels and exclusive resorts, fresh seafood and entertainment draw honeymooners to Manila and Cebu. Thailand and the Philippines compete for the Republic of Korea's honeymoon travel market via package travel advertisement. The recommendations of friends and relatives are not as influential in comparison to other destinations. In the table below, respondents' first and second responses to a multiple response survey indicates that leisure or relaxation is also a second purpose for most Korean visitors to the Philippines.

The Purpose of Travel (%)

	1st Choice	2nd Choice
Leisure/Relaxation	27.7	31.8
VFR	0.8	31.3
Business	31.2	1.7
Convention	13.4	3.3
Training	9.3	31.9
Culture/Sports	0.8	–
Honeymoon	4.3	–
Others	12.5	–

Source: Analysis from KTO's raw data (2006)

Travellers to the Philippines who reported their purpose of visit as pleasure also reported their main purpose for visiting the Philippines as a place that they had specifically wanted to visit. Almost 30% made this their first response and almost 27% of visitors indicated there is no difference in travel cost, compared to domestic travel as a second response. The table below details the types of responses indicated by pleasure travellers to the Philippines. Pleasure travellers to the Philippines reported engaging in a number of activities, including the enjoyment of natural scenery and city sightseeing.

The Main Reason of Travel (%)

	1st Choice	2nd Choice
There is no difference in travel cost, compared to domestic travel	27.0	12.0
Almost I have visited destination in Republic of Korea	3.4	8.4
A place that I want to visit	29.9	27.0
Not many tourist attractions in theRepublic of Korea	1.7	1.7
Sense of satisfaction with overseas travel	21.1	23.8
Not many entertainment facilities inRepublic of Korea	0.9	2.7
Having opportunities for group travel	16.0	3.4
Total	**100.0**	–

Source: Analysis from KTO's raw data (2006)

Activities for Pleasure Travellers to the Philippines (%)

Natural Scenery	20.9
Historic Monuments	9.0
Cultural Events/Festivals	5.6
Hot Springs	1.5
Nightlife/Entertainment	10.8
Swimming/Sunbathing	9.2
Hiking/Camping	0.9
Golf	1.2

Casino	1.7
City Sightseeing	19.0
Business	0.4
Shopping	19.2
Others	0.6

Source: Analysis from KTO's raw data (2006)

Package vs. FIT

The choice of travel type by outbound tourists to the Philippines is the package travel type. There are much more package travellers as indicated below.

Travel Type (%)

Independent Travel	32.7
Package Travel	67.3
Total	**100.0**

Source: Analysis from KTO's raw data (2006)

The specific type of travel to the Philippines for Koreans is largely package travel. The range of specific types of travel to the Philippines is honeymooners and student language training.

Satisfaction rate

Korean visitors to the Philippines generally reported satisfaction with their overall visit, and only a very small number of respondents reported being dissatisfied.

Korean visitors to the Philippines reported various degrees of satisfaction and dissatisfaction depending upon the tourism sector. The degree of satisfaction or dissatisfaction by sector is detailed in the tables below: accommodation, food, shopping items, tour guide's service, and tour itinerary. Korean visitors to the Philippines generally reported being satisfied with their experience in terms of all these sectors.

Satisfaction Level by Sector (%)

	Accommodation	Food	Shopping Items	Guide Service	Tour Itinerary and Contents
Very satisfied	10.8	9.3	5.5	11.9	9.8
Somewhat satisfied	69.4	45.1	54.3	42.2	66.3
Neutral	11.1	40.2	30.4	21.8	19.5
Somewhat dissatisfied	4.3	5.4	5.4	1.1	1.1
Very dissatisfied	0.0	0.0	1.1	0.0	0.0
I don't know	4.4	0.0	3.3	23.0	3.3

Travel inconveniences

Korean visitors to the Philippines largely indicated the language barrier as the major travel inconvenience encountered during their visit. The second major inconvenience was food, but most people indicated that they encountered no travel inconvenience. All 14 kinds of travel inconvenience are listed below:

Travel Inconveniences (%)

Language Barrier	26.6
Money Exchange	1.8
Airplane Reservation	1.8
Information Desk Service	3.6
Local Transportation	9.0
Forced Employee Tips	6.0
Forced Selling	4.2
Nightlife/Entertainment	0.6
Food	13.8
Criminal/Safety	5.4
Forced the additional Expenditure of Travel Agency	2.4
Guide Tips	3.0
Airplane Transfer	1.2
Change of Itinerary	0.6
Nothing	20.0

Source: Analysis from KTO's raw data (2006)

3.1.9 Thailand

Existing traffic and traffic patterns

Thailand is traditionally a stable destination for Korean outbound travellers. 661,779 people visited Thailand in 2005. However, even though more female Koreans are traveling abroad, there are slightly more Korean males visiting Thailand. The following table indicates the total numbers, percentage change and percentage share of Korean departures by gender to Thailand from 2001 to 2005.

Korean Departures by Gender to Thailand, 2001-2005

Year	Total		Male			Female		
	Number	+/- (%)	Number	+/- (%)	Share (%)	Number	+/- (%)	Share (%)
2001	446,886	27.3	232,569	27.1	52.0	214,317	27.5	48.0
2002	581,514	30.1	298,135	28.2	51.3	283,379	32.2	48.7
2003	575,154	-1.1	301,736	1.2	52.5	273,418	-3.5	47.5
2004	754,093	31.1	377,198	25.0	50.0	376,895	37.9	50.0
2005	661,779	-12.2	339,005	-10.1	51.2	322,774	-14.4	48.8

Source: Analysis from KTO's raw data (2006)

Koreans have consistently visited Thailand for pleasure much more than for any other reasons at least since 2001. As indicated in the table below, 565,772 travellers to Thailand indicated pleasure as the main purpose of their visit.

Growth of Korean Departures by Purpose to Thailand, 2001-2005

Category	2001		2002		2003		2004		2005	
	Number	+/- (%)	Number	+/- (%)	Number	+/- (%)	Number	+/- (%)	Number	+/- (%)
Pleasure	375,909	29.9	500,654	33.2	493,657	-1.4	666,673	35.1	565,772	-15.1
Business	41,998	18.8	44,275	5.4	47,032	6.2	49,378	5.0	49,323	-0.1
VFR*	11,812	-14.0	13,779	16.7	17,740	28.8	19,030	7.3	29.981	57.6
Official	581	49.0	838	44.2	927	10.6	780	-15.9	715	-8.3
Convention	2,768	19.2	3,249	17.4	2,390	-26.4	3,063	28.2	2,300	-24.9
Others	13,818	38.0	18,719	35.5	13,408	-28.4	15,169	13.1	13,688	-9.8

* Excluding crew members
Source: Analysis from KTO's raw data (2006)/

Most visitors to Thailand are people who are employed in the private sector or unemployed such as housewives and the retirees who make up a quickly growing demographic segment of the Republic of Korea's outbound tourist market. The following table illustrates the details of Korean departures by occupation to Thailand from 2001 to 2005.

Korean Departures by Occupation to Thailand, 2001-2005

Category	2001		2002		2003		2004		2005	
	Number	+/- (%)	Number	+/- (%)	Number	+/- (%)	Number	+/- (%)	Number	+/- (%)
Official	4,178	42.3	5,804	38.9	5,939	2.3	8,262	39.1	6,642	-19.6
Private Sector	–	–	208,859	–	203,548	-2.5	250,700	23.2	206,466	-17.6
Self Employed	27,150	36.1	36,948	36.1	37,553	1.6	42,160	12.3	36,181	-14.2
Educator	–	–	11,127	–	12,679	14.0	16,450	29.7	12,377	-24.8
Student	–	–	44,351	–	48,208	8.7	69,556	44.3	61,286	-11.9
Others	–	–	29,862	–	26,064	-12.7	31,268	20.0	25,613	-18.1
Unemployed	–	–	246,674	–	243,351	-1.3	338,327	39	315,448	-6.8

Source: Analysis from KTO's raw data (2006)

Most travellers to Thailand are in their twenties (169,885 for the year 2005), followed closely by those in their thirties and in their forties. The detailed breakdown of Korean departures by age to Thailand can be found the table below for the years 2001 to 2005.

Due to the tsunami disaster in the end of 2004, the number of honeymooners has decreased dramatically, showing 15.2% decline in 2005. Golf vacation enjoyed by 40s and 50s are also affected by this disaster.

Growth of Korean Departures by Age to Thailand, 2001-2005

Category	2001		2002		2003		2004		2005	
	Number	+/- (%)	Number	+/- (%)	Number	+/- (%)	Number	+/- (%)	Number	+/- (%)
0 – 20	36,604	50.1	49,390	34.9	55,201	11.8	75,017	36.0	67,827	-9.6
21 – 30	139,601	19.0	162,349	16.3	143,974	-11.3	200,329	39.1	169,885	-15.2
31 – 40	103,571	30.2	134,278	29.7	133,188	-0.8	172,962	29.9	153,469	-11.3
41 – 50	80,271	32.3	114,356	42.5	124,179	8.6	152,648	22.9	136,263	-10.7
51 – 60	59,428	23.5	79,786	34.3	78,086	-2.1	102,688	31.5	89,663	-12.7
> 61	29,121	29.8	43,466	49.3	42,714	-1.7	53,079	24.3	46,906	-11.6

Source: Analysis from KTO's raw data (2006)

The following data was obtained from interviews with tour operators, travel agencies and airlines, and Korean representative of Thailand Tourism Authority (TAT) as well as related websites.

Evaluation of Existing Traffic and Traffic Pattern in Thailand

Category	Contents		
Ease of entry	• Visa free entry		
Accommodation	• Wide variety of accommodation at all levels • Ongoing new hotel development • Low prices by international standards		
Local transportation	• Sufficient domestic flights for transfers • Good local transportations but congestion is common • Affordable and safe • Sky train and water taxi make Bangkok accessible		
Health, medical and insurance facilities	• High quality, affordable health care • Opportunity for wellness tourism		
Security	• Bangkok and northern Thailand are seen as safe • Phuket and southern Thailand are not seen as safe		
Food	• Good variety of food • Hygiene is acceptable		
Telecommunications	• High standard • Roaming is not a problem		
Recreation and entertainment	• Wide variety of activities available for tourists • Urban tourism attractions, shopping, sightseeing, etc • Spa tourism is growing • Many night markets and night life activities		
Tour products	• Honeymoon for Bangkok, Pattaya, Phuket • Golf Tour		
Flight Schedule	Route	Korean Airline	Asiana Airline
	Incheon – Bangkok	15 flights/week	25 flights/week
	Incheon – Phuket	2 flights/week	4 flights/week
	Incheon – Pattaya	18 flights/week	9 flights/week

Factors affecting destination selection

For Koreans, major information sources affecting the decision to travel to Thailand include prices, business reasons, or the availability of NTO promotions. "Word of mouth" is one of main factors affecting destinations selection. NTO's brand slogans such as "Amazing Thailand", "Eternal allure that awakens a new millennium", "Be my guest, Thailand", "Experience true value", and "Wellbeing" are effective in the Republic of Korea. Interestingly, low price incurred when traveling to Thailand was not considered as a main factor by Korean travellers. Korean travellers tend to show a higher level of perceived service value. All major factors affecting the travel decision and travel information source are listed below:

Factors Affecting Destination Selection (%)

Package Travel Advertisement	50.4
NTO Promotion Activities	2.1
Friends/Relatives Recommendation	28.2
Internet Search	8.6
Favorable Image towards Destination	5.3
Low Price	2.1
Business Related	3.3
Total	**100.0**

Source: Analysis from KTO's raw data (2006)

The main travel information source is travel agency (56.2%), followed by the internet (22.4%), recommendation from experienced travellers (18.2%), travel magazines and guidebooks:

Travel Information Sources (%)

Travel Agency	56.2
People with Overseas Travel Experiences	18.2
Internet	22.4
Travel Magazines and Guidebooks	3.2
Total	**100.0**

Source: Analysis from KTO's raw data (2006)

Purpose of travel

Outbound tourists bound for Thailand reported their main purpose of visit as leisure or relaxation as can be seen in the table below:

Purpose of Travel (%)

Leisure/Relaxation/Recreation	89.1
VFR	1.1
Business and Specialized activities	3.3
Religion and Pilgrimage	2.2
Voluntary Service Activities	4.3

Source: Analysis from KTO's raw data (2006)

Travellers to Thailand who reported their purpose of visit as pleasure also reported their main purpose for visiting Thailand because "Korean perceived overseas travel to Thailand as no difference in travel cost, compared with domestic travel". The table below details the types of responses indicated by pleasure travellers to Thailand:

The Main Reason of Travel (%)

	1st Choice	2nd Choice
There is no difference in travel cost, compared to domestic travel	36.8	12.0
I have visited almost all destinations in theRepublic of Korea	2.9	4.3
A place that I want to visit	19.4	21.7
Not many tourist attractions in theRepublic of Korea	5.4	1.1
Sense of satisfaction with overseas travel	24.8	38.0
Having opportunities for group travel	10.7	4.3

Source: Analysis from KTO's raw data (2006)

Pleasure travellers to Thailand reported engaging in a number of activities including sightseeing natural scenery (100%), followed by visiting historic monuments (80.4%), swimming and sunbathing (40.2%), participating in cultural events and festivals (23.9%). The 10 most frequently indicated activities are listed below:

Activities for Pleasure Travellers to Thailand (%)

Activities	(%)
Natural Scenery	100.0
Visiting historic monuments	80.4
Cultural Events/Festivals	23.9
Hot Springs	3.3
Nightlife/Entertainment	10.9
Swimming/Sunbathing	40.2
Hiking/Camping	1.1
Golf	2.2
City Sightseeing	29.3
Shopping	27.2

Source: Analysis from KTO's raw data (2006)

Package vs. FIT

Choices of travel type by outbound tourists to Thailand favor the package travel (80.4%) rather than the independent travel type (19.6%).

Satisfaction rate

Korean visitors to Thailand generally reported satisfaction with their overall visit. In fact, over 68.3% of visitors were at least somewhat satisfied, and only a very small number of respondents reported being dissatisfied.

The main reasons for being dissatisfied are related to both forced guide tips and unpleasant employees. Korean visitors to Thailand reported various degrees of satisfaction and dissatisfaction depending upon the tourism sector. The degree of satisfaction or dissatisfaction by sector is detailed in the tables below: accommodation, food, shopping items, tour guide's service, tour itinerary and contents. Korean visitors to Thailand generally reported being satisfied with their experience in terms of all these sectors. However, "shopping items" and "guide services" are relatively reported with a lower level of satisfaction perceived by Korean visitors to Thailand. These sectors should be improved consistently, in collaboration with both Thailand and the Republic of Korea.

Satisfaction Level by Sector (%)

	Accommodation	Food	Shopping Items	Guide Service	Tour Itinerary and Contents
Very satisfied	10.9	4.4	2.1	10.8	2.2
Somewhat satisfied	64.1	58.7	2.2	12.0	64.1
Neutral	21.7	21.7	67.4	52.2	31.5
Somewhat dissatisfied	3.3	14.1	25.0	21.7	2.2
Very dissatisfied	0.0	1.1	3.3	3.3	0.0

Travel inconveniences

Korean visitors to Thailand generally indicated the language barrier as the major travel inconvenience encountered during their visit. Food was the second major travel inconvenience indicated, while 15.2% of respondents indicated that they encountered no travel inconvenience.

3.1.10 Vietnam

Existing traffic and traffic patterns

Vietnam is one of the favorite destinations in the Asian region for Korean outbound travellers. 268,110 people or 31.9% of the republic of Korea's outbound market visited Vietnam in 2005. The table below indicates the total numbers, percentage change and percentage share of Korean departures by gender to Vietnam from 2001 to 2005.

Korean Departures by Gender to Vietnam, 2001-2005

Year	Total		Male			Female		
	Number	+/- (%)	Number	+/- (%)	Share (%)	Number	+/- (%)	Share (%)
2001	60,498	42.2	46,417	37.4	76.7	14,081	60.9	23.3
2002	90,885	50.2	67,530	45.5	74.3	23,355	65.9	25.7
2003	112,673	24.0	79,642	17.9	70.7	33,031	41.4	29.3
2004	203,300	80.4	126,790	59.2	62.4	76,510	131.6	37.6
2005	268,110	31.9	165,820	30.8	61.9	102,290	33.7	38.1

Source: Analysis from KTO's raw data (2006)

Koreans have consistently visited Vietnam for business rather than pleasure since 2001. As indicated in the following table 37.5% of travellers to Vietnam indicated pleasure as the main purpose of their visit.

Growth of Korean Departures by Purpose to Vietnam, 2001-2005

Category	2001		2002		2003		2004		2005	
	Number	+/- (%)	Number	+/- (%)	Number	+/- (%)	Number	+/- (%)	Number	+/- (%)
Pleasure	23,968	94.8	41,222	72.0	59,220	43.7	138,687	134.2	190,718	37.5
Business	28,741	18.4	39,214	36.4	41,611	6.1	46,762	12.4	50,752	8.5
VFR*	4,058	16.7	5,433	33.9	6,634	22.1	10,259	54.6	17,435	70.0
Official	345	12.4	393	13.9	384	-2.3	616	60.4	628	2.0
Convention	419	14.5	599	43.0	456	-23.9	872	91.2	917	5.2
Others	2,967	51.3	4,024	35.6	4,368	8.6	6,104	39.7	7,660	25.5

* Excluding crew members
Source: Analysis from KTO's raw data (2006)

Most visitors to Vietnam are unemployed, although this number is followed closely by those who are employed in the private sector. The table below illustrates the details of Korean departures by occupation to Vietnam from 2001 to 2005.

Korean Departures by Occupation to Vietnam, 2001-2005

Category	2001		2002		2003		2004		2005	
	Number	+/- (%)	Number	+/- (%)	Number	+/- (%)	Number	+/- (%)	Number	+/- (%)
Official	699	135.4	845	20.9	1,209	43.1	2,935	142.8	4,004	36.4
Private Sector	–	–	45,924	–	51,977	13.2	76,292	46.8	91,870	20.4
Self Employed	6,931	63.1	9,443	36.2	11,816	25.1	19,295	63.3	26,818	39.0
Educator	–	–	2,178	–	3,056	40.3	5,833	90.9	7,326	25.6
Student	–	–	3,732	–	4,751	27.3	8,626	81.6	11,638	34.9
Others	–	–	4,472	–	4,779	6.9	9,399	96.7	11,241	19.6
Unemployed	–	–	4,846	–	35,691	43.7	81,768	129.1	116,114	42.0

Source: Analysis from KTO's raw data (2006)

Most travellers to Vietnam are in their forties (83,654 for the year 2005), followed closely by those in their fifties and in their thirties. The detailed breakdown of Korean departures by age to Vietnam can be found in the following table for the years 2001 to 2005.

Growth of Korean Departures by Age to Vietnam, 2001-2005

Category	2001		2002		2003		2004		2005	
	Number	+/- (%)	Number	+/- (%)	Number	+/- (%)	Number	+/- (%)	Number	+/- (%)
0 – 20	2,811	27.0	3,717	32.2	5,048	35.8	9,905	96.2	14,984	51.3
21 – 30	6,765	32.7	9,216	36.2	10,243	11.1	18,249	78.2	22,888	25.4
31 – 40	17,430	30.4	24,626	41.3	27,570	12.0	43,409	57.5	56,257	29.6
41 – 50	19,381	43.2	30,025	54.9	37,278	24.2	63,161	69.4	83,654	32.5
51 – 60	10,141	59.9	15,725	55.0	21,960	39.7	45,969	109.3	60,739	32.1
>61	4,257	94.7	8,131	91.0	11,180	37.5	23,455	109.8	30,489	30.0

Source: Analysis from KTO's raw data (2006)

The following information was obtained from interviews with tour operators, travel agencies and airlines, and Korean representative of Vietnam National Tourism Administration as well as related websites.

Existing Traffic and Traffic Patterns in Vietnam

Category	Contents		
Ease of entry	• Visa on Arrival		
Accommodation	• Various kinds of accommodation • Low priced hotel to luxury hotel or resort		
Local transportation	• Bicycle and motorcycle for main transfer • Inconvenient transportation system		
Health, medical and insurance facilities	• Mineral water recommended for drinking		
Security	• Underdeveloped medical industry • Many pick-pockets		
Food	• Rice and rice noodles are the staple		
Telecommunications	• Growing telecommunication industry		
Recreation and entertainment	• Night clubs		
Tour products	• Ho Cho Minh City tour • Honeymoon for Ha Long Bay, Hanoi		
Flight Schedule	**Route**	**Korean Airline**	**Asiana Airline**
	Incheon – Hanoi	14 flights/week	7 flights/week
	Incheon – HoChiMinh City	8 flights/week	5 flights/week

Source: Korean Airline, Asiana Airline, Embassy of Vietnam in the Republic of Korea, JNTO

Factors affecting destination selection

For Koreans, the major decision to travel to Vietnam is for business purposes. Korean travellers to Vietnam reported the recommendations of people with overseas travel experiences as the major factor affecting their travel decision.

Korean visitors to Vietnam almost unanimously indicated the language barrier as the major travel inconvenience encountered during their visit. Information while touring was the second major travel inconvenience. But most Koreans reported an overall sense of satisfaction while traveling to Vietnam

Chapter 4

Recommendations

Several key Asia Pacific countries have been identified in this report as popular destinations for Koreans who travel abroad. Among the 10,077,619 outbound travellers reported last year, about 73% of them visited the Asia Pacific destinations. This trend should continue through 2006 due to an increasingly strong Korean currency as well as other aspects of Korean national economic growth. Future research regarding the Korean tourism market should focus on further improvements to the existing product to enhance its value to the inbound destination. Destination countries should adopt and implement certain policies, strategies and marketing programs that can potentially increase traffic from the Republic of Korea. Certain changes to rectify shortcomings in destination markets should be implemented to satisfy Korean travellers. In addition, destination markets based on market intelligence on the Korean outbound tourism market should create certain public relation programs and advertising campaigns.

Korean outbound travellers reported language as the major inconvenience when traveling overseas, in particular to Asian destinations. It is recommended that signage on the streets and dining menus in Korean should be provided. To attract more Korean travellers to certain destinations, Asian destinations should pay attention to the following marketing strategies and policy implications:

4.1 Marketing Strategies

4.1.1 Destination Brand Awareness

Koreans tend to perceive Asian destinations differently based on their experience. The following perceptual map can be employed to evaluate Korean's perceptions toward Asian destinations. It can help each travel destination in Asia establish policies and marketing strategies for improving its destination brand awareness.

Perceptual Map

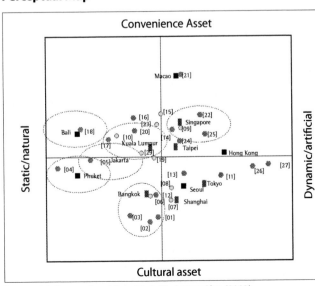

01) A lot to see; 02) Interesting; 03) Can feel the local customs; 04) Beautiful natural scenery; 05) Attractive place for ecological sightseeing; 06) Historic remains/sites to visit; 07) Unique architectural attributes; 08) Many special events and celebrations; 09) Various entertainment; 10) Various recreational activities; 11) Convenient shopping; 12) Availability of various specialty products; 13) Different/unique cuisine; 14) Travel convenient; 15) Safe; 16) Pleasant weather; 17) Peaceful and pleasant place; 18) Suitable for elderlies; 19) You get to experience more than what you bargain for; 20) Friendly locals; 21) Easy to communicate with locals; 22) Convenient transportation for tourist spot; 23) No complications in coming into the country; 24) Various lodging facilities to choose from; 25) Various forms of transportation; 26) Nice place to conduct business; 27) Suitable for international conference.

Source: Jeju International Free City's Marketing Plan (2003)

4.1.2 E-Marketing

Because the source of travel information is largely "word of mouth" influenced by people with overseas travel experience, it is very important to satisfy opinion leaders. It is recommended that destination establishes "Customer Relation Management (CRM) to take care of the influential people. Moreover, internet is an important source of travel information for Korean travellers. E-marketing is recommended to enhance destination image or awareness to attract more Korean outbound travellers.

E-marketing will be a powerful tool for advertising specific destinations for Korean travellers. This market is emotional and value-oriented. Destination homepages can influence Korean's travel decision-making process. Destination homepage should have the following elements to attract more clients and make profits:

- content;
- context;
- commerce;
- community;
- customization;
- communication;
- connection.

E-marketing should focus on the process of implementation strategies which include Korean customer acquisition, Korean customer cultivation, and Korean customer retention. Korean customer acquisition is seeking for potential Korean visitors, based on their travel experience, age preference, etc. Korean customer cultivation relates to what they need and how to encourage them to purchase services or products. New travel products should be developed and provided through destination websites. Korean customer retention focuses on how to create repeat Korean visitors. Because Korean overseas travellers expressed higher level of satisfaction when experiencing most Asian destination, as survey results indicated, each Asian destination management organization (DMO) should develop an effective management tool to create repeat Korean visitors. CRM (customer relationship management) should be developed for implementing e-marketing strategies.

4.1.3 STP (Segmenting-Targeting-Positioning) Strategies

The Republic of Korea's tourism destination countries should closely consider the specific market segmentation of Korean outbound tourists. In addition, destination countries should consider the special needs and characteristics of major market segments when generating segmenting-targeting-positioning strategies. For example, as mentioned previously, certain major destinations such as China, Japan and the United States of America should more closely examine the characteristics of certain outbound tourism market segments of the Republic of Korea. Regarding Japan, certain market segments such as women and the "unemployed" can be interpreted as a market segment, namely, housewives, a potential target market that has grown 34.1% since 2002. The elderly or aging strata have also enjoyed a greater growth of 33.69% for those in their 50s and 31.6% for those in their 60s.

4.1.4 FAM (Familiarization) Trips

Another effective marketing approach for those wishing to target the Republic of Korea's outbound tourism market are familiarization trips. FAM trips are travel products that are offered to special opinion leaders or representatives of a particular travel market. The Republic of Korea has effectively employed FAM trips in the past to draw special market interests. Of note is the Korean Wave, a series of media events or programs that generated a great interest in the Republic of Korea, specifically in certain Asian countries like Japan, Hong Kong, Singapore and China. The Republic of Korea capitalized upon the presence of the Korean Wave by offering certain programs for journalists or other special interest groups. FAM trips are also usually offered to operators or travel agents in order to 'familiarize' them with special features associated with the destination. Destination countries interested in the Korean outbound market can consider implementing some FAM trips as demonstrated by the Republic of Korea.

4.1.5 PR Activities

Various PR activities associated with more general trends or events can be very effective in generating a specific market demand for an equally specific interest. As mentioned above, the Korean wave generated a widespread following in Japan, Hong Kong, Singapore and China, and to capitalize on this, the republic of Korea developed tourism products that would cater to this market's needs. The Republic of Korea also became the site of several media events using stars of the Korean Wave to promote various destinations in the Republic of Korea as authentic cultural tourism destinations. Certain influential media representatives have also been invited to the Republic of Korea to enjoy particular destinations and products in order to develop a targeted market interest accessible only through those media representatives' readership. Destination countries interested in the Korean outbound tourism market can consider implementing some of these PR activities in order to increase arrivals from the Republic of Korea.

4.1.6 Support of Destination Representatives in the Republic of Korea

Many representatives from international tourism organizations are based in the Republic of Korea. These branch offices represent the interests of another country in the Republic of Korea's tourism market. Specifically, these organizations like Japan National Tourism Organization (JNTO), China National Tourism Administration (CNTA), Hong Kong Tourism Board (HKTB) and Singapore Tourism Promotion Board (STPB) all strive to provide a wide range of promotional materials and special events that will draw Korean tourists to their respective countries. The Republic of Korea continues to support their efforts through policy and practice, namely via the administrative body of the Ministry of Culture and Tourism.

4.1.7 Incentive and Corporate Meeting Markets

Multinational companies are increasingly using international tours as corporate incentive programs. In the past, these corporations would choose resort areas as destinations. But as the Republic of Korea is becoming more and more industrialized, therefore corporate meeting markets are shifting to destinations such as Singapore, Hong Kong and Australia. Destinations interested in targeting this potentially lucrative market should focus on developing awareness and products that cater to this market's special needs.

4.2 Bilateral Tourism Exchange Program

Bilateral tourism exchange programs are an effective method for increasing tourism traffic from the Republic of Korea. Destination countries who host Korean travel market segments can increase their share by implementing bilateral tourism exchange programs. As illustrated in the following figure, bilateral tourism exchange programs are effective when the facilitation of tourism is standardized among destinations, when information regarding tourism is shared among travel promotion offices, when exchange and assistance regarding facilities and cities and natural resources occurs, when education and training regarding tourism is developed, when statistics and research are shared, and when tourism safety and security are promoted. Bilateral tourism exchange programs can be instrumental in the regional development of Korean outbound tourism.

Bilateral Tourism Exchange Program Model

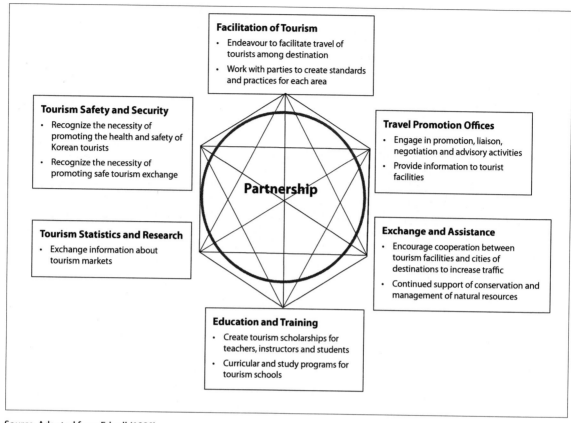

Source: Adapted from Edgell (1999)

Bibliography

Asia-Pacific Economic Cooperation (2002), *Application of E-commerce Strategies to Small and Medium Sized Tourism Enterprises (SMTEs) in the APEC Region.*

Bank of Korea (2006), *Currency Rate Fluctuation.*

Edgell, D. L. (1999), *Tourism Policy: The Next Millennium,* Sagamore Publishing, Champaign, IL.

Ministry of Construction and Transportation (2006), *Transportation Information.*

Ministry of Culture and Tourism (2005), *Annual Report on Korean Tourism,* MCT.

Korea Tourism Association (2006), *Current Information on Korean Travel Agencies,* KTA.

Korea Tourism Organization (2006), *A Study on Korean Outbound Market,* KTO.

http://www.bok.or.kr

http://www.knto.or.kr

http://www.koreatravel.or.kr

http://www.mct.go.kr

http://www.moct.go.kr

http://www.ngi.go.kr